The Shadow and the Counsellor

The psychological concept of the 'shadow' has not always been fully appreciated by those not grounded in analytical psychology. Yet an understanding of the potentially harmful aspects of themselves and of their professional role can be extremely useful to practitioners across the spectrum of therapeutic approaches, offering counsellors a means of comprehending their personal and professional experience.

Using examples from both personal and professional settings, *The Shadow and the Counsellor* introduces the concept of shadow, examines how it comes into being and explores its impact within the counselling context. It considers how the counsellor's work may be affected by identifying and incorporating material from the shadow into conscious awareness, and applies the concept of shadow to the role of counsellor and counselling itself.

The Shadow and the Counsellor should prove accessible to a broad spectrum of counsellors and therapists, challenging them to face those aspects of themselves and of the counselling role which can do harm as well as good.

Steve Page is Head of the Counselling Service at the University of Hull. He is co-author of *Supervising the Counsellor* (Routledge 1994).

The Shadow and the Counsellor

Working with darker aspects
of the person, role and profession

Steve Page

London and New York

First published in 1999 by Routledge
11 New Fetter Lane, London EC4P 4EE

Simultaneously published in the USA and Canada
by Routledge
29 West 35th Street, New York, NY 10001

Routledge is an imprint of the Taylor & Francis Group

Typeset in Goudy by Keystroke, Jacaranda Lodge, Wolverhampton
Printed and bound in Great Britain by Creative Print and Design
(Wales), Ebbw Vale

British Library Cataloging in Publication Data
A catalogue record for this book is available from the British Library

Library of Congress Cataloging in Publication Data
Page, Steve, 1955–
    The shadow and the counsellor / Steve Page.
        p.   cm.
    Includes bibliographical references (p. 000) and index.
    ISBN 0–415–13144–8 (hardcover). – ISBN 0–415–13145–6 (pbk.)
    1. Counselors. 2. Counseling. 3. Shadow (Psychoanalysis)
    I. Title.
BF637.C6P24   1999
158'.3–dc21   98–45952
                                                                  CIP

ISBN 0–415–13144–8 (hbk)
ISBN 0–415–13145–6 (pbk)

For Christine, Hannah and Dominic,
with thanks.

Contents

Illustrations

Figures

Table

Acknowledgements

I am very grateful to Christine Barker and Val Wosket who have read and made valuable comments upon a number of drafts of the whole manuscript. Christine, my partner, has been a tremendous source of support in all aspects of this project. I have also received helpful comments on parts of the text from Christopher Jarrell, Pamela MacDougall, Sue Montgomery and Fay Simpson. Although I have made alterations based on many of the comments that have been offered I remain responsible for all that I have written.

I wish to thank the many friends, colleagues, clients, trainers, course members, supervisors, supervisees and others who, over the years, have played a part in helping me formulate the thoughts that are contained in this book. Of those with whom I no longer have contact, some I remember with fondness, while others I can no longer recall at will although their influence remains. At the risk of offending some through omission I want to identify the following whose influence I have been aware of during the course of writing: Chris Bostock, Kate Carr, Eileen Clements, Mary Connor, Fabian Cowper, Christine Domegan, Peter Hawkins, Geoff Pelham, Brian Slater, Nick Totton, William West and Sue Williams.

There are many others who have provided assistance, support and encouragement in various forms, including members of my family and Elizabeth Adeline, Jackie and Andrew Close, Tim Gauntlett, Jill Hall, Linda Hastings, Peter and Philippa Melhuish, Robin Shohet, Phil Taylor, Denise Townsend, Tim Willson and Joan Wilmot. I am also grateful for the support I have received from colleagues at the University of Hull. Staff at the libraries of the University of Bradford and the University of Hull have been helpful in assisting with literature searches. The editorial staff at Routledge have been patient and encouraging throughout.

I wish to acknowledge all those clients, colleagues, supervisees, course members and friends whose experiences I have drawn on in the examples I use. Many I have not been able to ask directly for permission although where practicable I have sought and received consent to include examples based on the experience of specific people. I trust that for others the disguises I create are sufficient to ensure anonymity from all but the individuals themselves. I hope that any who do think that they recognise themselves in an example feel that I have been purposeful and respectful in the way that I have included their experience as this has been my intention. While many of the examples have been altered in various details they all have a basis in actual events.

Writing this book has had a healing effect upon me because I have faced and accepted a number of aspects of my own shadow in the process. I also recognise that there may be some who feel bruised by my manifestations of shadow over the years. I hope that any who do and come to read this book will find doing so restorative in some way.

Introduction

There was a moment with a client when I suddenly became aware that what I was saying could be understood to imply that I was above or beyond the everyday human struggles that she had been describing. My comment was seemingly innocuous, I simply said 'That must have been really hard for you' as she described a situation where she felt torn between the conflicting demands others were making of her. However, I recognised a flavour of superiority underlying the tone with which I delivered my supposedly empathic intervention. On hearing my own words in this way I was shocked, for I would not accept the suggestion that I consider myself to be free of the difficulties that others experience. To back up my view I would be able to cite examples of areas in my life that are at times problematic and unsatisfactory. Yet despite this knowledge of my own struggles, if I am to apply the honest self-reflection I would hope to see in others then I must accept that somewhere within my psyche lurks the belief that I am beyond such mundane matters. I must accept this because I heard my words as 'other' to how I perceive myself.

What am I to do with this piece of information? If left unchecked it might develop into an absurd and highly damaging fantasy: a belief that I am in some way omnipotent, beyond human vulnerability. Indeed, this sense of grandiosity may be growing outside of my conscious awareness and what a sorry figure I would then become. Added to the dangers this incipient belief may herald for me is the potential impact upon my client, for if I can hear my words in this manner so, presumably, can she. This could have a damaging effect upon her: it might drive her further into feeling herself to be inadequate, or increase her dependency upon me by fostering the belief that I am some sort of super-being to whom she must look up.

What am I to do? I do not support this belief consciously yet it would appear to exist within me. Furthermore, I work within a profession where others may perceive me in a somewhat distorted manner. In the role of counsellor[1] I am sometimes believed by the client to be some sort of human paragon who has worked out the secret of living a happy and fulfilled life. As a supervisor or trainer of other practitioners I may also be seen as the expert: the therapist who really knows what he is doing. These distorted perceptions of me, these projections,[2] serve to bolster the inflated view of myself and together form a potentially dangerous cocktail. However, I do not consider that I am being overly self-revealing in acknowledging this aspect of myself for it has been well recognised for some time that as counsellors we are all vulnerable to becoming over-inflated (Marmor 1953; Sharaf and Levinson 1964). Indeed Kottler has positioned this as a central danger for therapists: 'The principal hazard of our profession is the narcissistic belief that we really are special' (1986: 17). Furthermore, a certain degree of arrogance is implicit in our willingness to take on the role of facilitating growth, development or healing in others. What is in question then, is our level of awareness of this aspect of ourselves and the degree of success that we have in ensuring that it, along with other potentially destructive aspects of ourselves, does not do harm to our clients.

The incident with which I began can be described as an example of the personal shadow of the counsellor emerging in this therapeutic encounter. Carl Jung used 'shadow' as a psychological term to describe the 'dark aspects of the personality' (1959b: 14).[3] This description expresses the ambiguity inherent within the concept of shadow in terms of 'darkness'.[4] It can be associated with the unknown: that which is outside of the 'light' of conscious awareness. It can also be associated with that which is evil or harmful. I suggest that we take as a starting-point a working model of the shadow as a specific part of a larger personal unconscious, as indicated in Figure 1.

In this model, psychological material within the shadow is characterised by having the potential to be actively destructive or harmful. However, this is only a potential and it is not certain that it will ever be realised. It may never come to expression and it is possible for an aspect of shadow to be harnessed and directed in a purposeful and creative manner, although this is no small undertaking. I use the terms 'destructive' and 'harmful' in a pragmatic sense to describe apparent consequences, while recognising that it is hard to determine harm (Jenkins 1997) and that doing so is more a legal task than a therapeutic one. In the therapeutic field what matters most is that we recognise that harm can and does occur in human relationships, including counselling relationships.

In addition to the ambiguity of 'darkness' there is another quality inherent in the nature of shadow: it has a counterpart. In the physical plane a shadow only has existence as a consequence of light falling upon an object so that the shadow remains a secondary function of that object. To

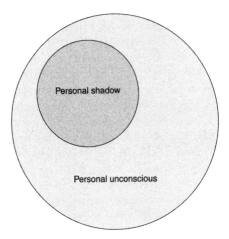

Figure 1 Shadow and the individual unconscious

this extent the psychological shadow function is analogous to the physical: it exists in relation to an 'other'. In this case the other comprises those conscious aspects of personality for which Jung (1971) used the term 'ego' and Rogers (1951) called the 'self structure'. We should be mindful that there are dangers in drawing parallels between the shadows we know within the physical realm and the psychological function of shadow. The shadow cast by light falling upon an object is a direct representation of that object. It may be distorted and broken up but essentially the shadow cast mirrors in two dimensions the three-dimensional object to which it relates. On the psychological plane the relationship between the ego and the shadow is decidedly more complex. The shadow is not merely a mirror of the ego, although there will be elements of the shadow that will have direct counterparts within the ego. There will also be other aspects of the shadow, the roots of which are not so readily visible within the consciously acknowledged aspects of personality.

I need to step back for a moment and acknowledge one of the challenges I face in writing this book that I recognise may in turn cause difficulties for some who read it. Like many of my colleagues in the counselling field in Britain I do not work from singular therapeutic orientation. My training and experience as a counsellor, which started in the mid-1970s, is multifaceted with influences across a broad range of approaches from the humanistic and psychodynamic traditions and includes work with individuals, groups and therapeutic communities. While there are strengths in this evolutionary process it does face me with a difficulty. I have no doubt that the concept of shadow is very appropriate for the issues I wish to address and is a notion with which I feel very comfortable (although I am far from comfortable when my own shadow actually manifests itself!). It would be possible to describe the incident with which I started this introduction in terms of the construction of personality that Rogers offers. In this he talks of those aspects of experience 'that is denied to awareness' (Rogers 1951: 529). However, Rogers frames his structure of personality within the 'here and now' phenomenological field. I want to explore the journey we undertake as people who are counsellors and the concept of shadow, reaching back as it does into our personal and collective history, seems to me a highly appropriate concept to use for this exploration. Nevertheless, I remain keenly aware that the notion of shadow belongs in a therapeutic tradition in which I can claim no particular knowledge or wealth of experience. Although the writings of Jung have been an influence upon me throughout my working life I am not steeped in the analytic psychology that its practitioners bring to bear. I feel very much that I am 'borrowing' the concept of shadow therefore and applying it to the experience of being a counsellor. I do so because the term shadow provides a means of naming aspects of experience that are important yet quite elusive. I do not consider that the term describes something fixed or rigid but rather something dynamic and changing. It is my hope that I shall encourage others from across the spectrum of therapeutic orientations, particularly those who have a similarly mixed therapeutic parentage to my own, to reflect upon their own practice. I recognise that this may well be highly unsatisfactory to others used to a singular therapeutic approach, but I fear that this cannot be helped.

The central core of this book is structured using a six-stage model for the relationship a counsellor may have with their shadow, with the first stage offering a way of understanding how the shadow comes into being. This model is offered as a framework, a means of considering the different attitudes we may take up from our conscious selves towards these unconscious aspects of who we are. Although it is presented as a linear sequence, because that is inherent in the written word, I am well aware that in reality we move about between the various stages and at any one time may occupy different places with regard to different elements of our shadow. Nevertheless there is, I believe, a recognisable movement through the different stages: from denial to recognition, then confrontation and incorporation. The possibility of the shadow guiding us in our work emerges only when these earlier stages have been experienced to a sufficient extent.

I include quite a number of notes to explain terms I use in the text or expand on an aspect of what I say in passing. Some of the terms I use are from analytic psychology, but others are from the physical sciences as I find these offer useful analogies for some of the processes in the therapeutic field.

I anticipate that as you read this book you may well stumble across elements of your own shadow. You may provide yourself with clues that this has occurred through feelings that suddenly come upon you such as anger, sadness or fear, or sensations of drowsiness or lack of concentration. Should this occur I urge you to be gentle and accepting for if you drift into disapproval or self-criticism you will push your growing insight away once more. I consider it inevitable that my shadow will find ways to express itself in the text. I do not simply mean in the consciously chosen examples, some of which are indeed autobiographical. Rather, it will appear in the choices I make about what is presented and what is not, how I explore the material and the biases that I inevitably apply. I ask that when you come across evidence of my shadow at work you will take up a similarly compassionate and generous attitude towards your discovery.

1 Counsellor: person, shadow and mask

As counsellors we are a curious collection, no two the same and yet possessing identifiable characteristics that are common among the majority if not all. Each of us brings the unique emotional, physical, psychological, social and spiritual aspects of who we are and takes on the set of purposes, qualities and attributes that go to make up the role that is described as counselling. We might think of this as each person who becomes a counsellor donning the suit of clothes that form the role. The person will be affected by the clothes they are wearing and similarly the attire will appear differently on each individual. To add to the diversity there are a range of outfits available, from the collared worsted wool of the formal practitioner through to the comfortable track suits favoured by those with a more casual style.

It is inevitable that who we are as people will be a highly significant influence upon our work with clients, in some cases the pivotal factor. To illustrate this let us consider the example of Ruth, a client who is struggling to decide how to move forward in a marriage that she experiences as quite oppressive and restrictive although still rich in many ways. Now let us imagine two counsellors Ruth might encounter. The first counsellor has herself come through a great struggle to find her sense of freedom and autonomy as a woman, ending her marriage during this process. The other counsellor has worked very hard to sustain and nurture her own long-term relationship which is now stable and fulfilling. It would be very surprising if there was no nuance of difference between how these two counsellors would interact with Ruth. Indeed it is a fairly absurd proposition: the counsellors' personal experience will inevitably have some impact. That is not to say that each would necessarily espouse the path they have them-selves chosen, it is rather more complex than that. There may be illicit encouragement in that direction, but there might equally be compensatory discouragement. There may be no clear influence towards one course of action or another, but it is not possible for the counsellors' own experience not to play some part in the relationship with Ruth. While every effort may be genuinely made to remain dispassionate and facilitative, in the final analysis the fate of Ruth's marriage may hinge on counsellor selection. Ruth is highly unlikely to have any direct knowledge of her counsellor's own experiences in relationships, and self-disclosure on the part of the counsellor is certainly not a satisfactory solution in such a situation (Segal 1993; Weiner 1978). If either counsellor did describe her own experience it would almost certainly undermine the effectiveness of the counselling work from the outset. This influencing component cannot be removed or neutralised but remains a function of the relational nature of the counselling process. It is integral to the wealth of human experience that each counsellor brings to the therapeutic relationship that is vital to the maturity and, it is to be hoped, wisdom that the counsellor possesses. As therapeutic work takes place within the context of a human relationship the personhood of the counsellor will remain a highly significant factor. Its impact is variable and to some extent unpredictable, although each of us may come to recognise the profile of our own influence as we gain in experience. We might start this process by considering what brought us into counselling in the first place.

MOTIVATION FOR BECOMING A COUNSELLOR

Choosing any career is inevitably a result of a number of factors and the decision, if deliberate decision it is, to become a counsellor or therapist is no different in this regard. One strongly influential component is that emulsion of genetic makeup and formative life experiences that results in the constitution of the individual personality. Out of this will develop a psychological nature that predisposes some to this work while others will be better prepared for other fields. Attempts have been made to study the variables that prepare the person for the possibility of being a counsellor, with Guy (1987) offering a particularly systematic view. He includes motivators such as inquisitiveness, introspection, capacity (and perhaps desire) for self-denial, desire for intimate contact, loneliness, desire for power and love and innate rebelliousness. He places these and other motivators in conjunction with the influence of the family of origin (Racusin *et al.* 1981) to provide a thorough examination. These issues are particularly important to those considering this work or involved in the assessment and selection of candidates suitable for the profession. Guy also emphasises that not all who are drawn to the profession are in fact suited to the work, citing the sobering study by Walfish *et al.* (1985) which found that among a sample of clinical psychologists close to half of those who had been in practice for more than ten years stated that they would not select this work if making the choice again. For those of us who are already in the field it can be illuminating to reflect in some detail on our own personal history and how this may have inclined us to this work, as illustrated by Heppner (1989). Such reflection, when undertaken honestly, is likely to be a revealing process and one that we can usefully undertake at various stages during our career as different aspects are likely to catch our attention each time.

In addition to our personal predisposition there will be an element of chance involved in the process. This serendipitous aspect of becoming a counsellor might involve a chance meeting, the right mentor, an influential book, a needy friend or a timely course. Each of these can be thought of as an activator:[1] triggering into action the potential that has thus far lain dormant. It is the combination of these two factors – the personal predisposition and the right activator – that results in someone choosing the counselling profession. There are many who have characteristics that make them appropriate for this work who will simply never be attracted to it; Guy terms such people the 'Suited but Not Interested' (1987: 25). They will be found moving off in some different direction, perhaps touched by an activator for some other line of work. Those who do gravitate towards the role of counsellor will bring with them a range of motivating factors, some of which will be known to that individual, while others remain unconscious.

It is possible, as Bugental (1964) has done, to split these factors into two groups: those that are appropriate in as much as they work in the interests of both practitioner and client and those that are inappropriate by virtue of using the client to gratify the needs of the counsellor. However, there are dangers in creating lists that define some characteristics as inherently 'good' and others as inherently 'bad'. It is not difficult to identify a number of motivational factors that sound laudable. Examples include: the desire to do work that feels worthwhile; curiosity about what makes people tick; a fascination with finding solutions; a sense of compassion towards the suffering of others; the wish to be a positive influence in the lives of others; a desire to use one's power and experience in the service of others and so on. However, I suspect that any one of these, or any other reason for choosing this type of work, can be double-edged: can be of either benefit or detriment to the client.

I am, with the wisdom of hindsight, well aware that one of the factors that drew me into this field is the opportunity it provides for well-contained intimate contact with others. This attraction has been fuelled by my ambivalence about being intimate and open in my relationships. I have a strong desire to be close and can easily be frustrated and then bored when

I find contact with the other person to be superficial or distant. In contrast I am also afraid that I will be engulfed, lose a sense of my separate self in my relationships. Thus, the intimacy of the counselling situation where I can have intense empathic contact with another person within predetermined boundaries of time and space while disclosing little about myself beyond my experience in the moment is a very attractive solution to my intimacy dilemma. I do not believe this need, which is being met daily in my counselling work, is inherently good or bad. For some clients my need dovetails well with what they are seeking from our counselling relationship. My desire for contact can draw clients deeper into the relationship despite, for example, their fear of trusting others. Alongside this I can utilise my low tolerance threshold for superficiality in order to cut through the smoke screening and rationalising distraction that some individuals create because of their trepidation about engaging with the more emotional aspects of their experience. However, there are times when these same desires of mine can overwhelm the other person if allowed to go unchecked. I am well aware that my clients may find me to be intrusive or emotionally demanding in my approach. This can lead to defences being further fortified and the client becoming increasingly inaccessible. There is then no inherent absolute judgement about the therapeutic impact of this particular need. Rather there are some for whom my need is a benefit, others for whom it is a potential liability.

Some time ago I saw a client who was strongly denying the distress he felt about the death of his mother. I could feel his pain and I wanted to reach out through his defences, to bridge the gap between us. However, I held back because I felt uncomfortable about this course of action: I was cautioned by the client's wariness of me. Exploring this in supervision it was apparent that this client was highly vulnerable and his defences brittle. It seemed imperative that the client was invited to explore beyond his defences, but having proffered this invitation it was my task to then wait patiently upon his decision. At times this was intensely frustrating for me but nevertheless remained, in my view and that of my supervisor, what he needed from me. For this particular client my personal needs inclined me to act in a way that was inappropriate to his therapeutic process. Had I not been aware of this tendency in me it is probable that I would have acted accordingly and frightened the client. This is but one example of the manner in which the motivations that drive each counsellor to be in this work can be either compatible or not to the work with a specific client.

Hillman (1979) offers a useful distinction between a need, which while seeking fulfilment can be recognised and contained, and a demand that requires satisfaction. A need that the counsellor has recognised and is able to contain does not necessarily threaten the efficacy of the therapeutic work. A demand that remains outside conscious awareness and will not let up until satisfied will affect the therapeutic process and may lead to the client being exploited or harmed. The capacity of the counsellor to recognise the need is a matter of self-awareness, for without awareness it may well continue to operate as an unconscious demand. Being able to recognise the need is in turn influenced by its potency: the degree of psychic energy fuelling it. The more potent or intense the need the more intra-personal defensive strategies are likely to be employed in order to maintain its unconscious status. Neither of these two factors is necessarily fixed. As we gain insight and self-understanding through our own thera-peutic and developmental work so the hitherto unconscious demands become increasingly visible and decreasingly intense. Let us not then delude ourselves that the recognition and management of a need is a simple process or indeed one that is assured of success. Some of these needs have considerable power, driven as they are by the potent emotional charge of many years of frustration and repression. Indeed some individuals are drawn to the role of counsellor, but their level of neediness is such that it is almost certain that they will fail in this endeavour.

It has been suggested by Gilbert *et al.* that those who are 'compulsively self-reliant, emotionally defended, or with severe narcissistic difficulties' (1989: 6) are not suited for the profession of psychotherapy and these exclusions also have relevance to counselling. These are each descriptions of people who are not going to be able to engage in or sustain effective therapeutic relationships. Someone who is compulsively self-reliant is not willing to engage in a mutual relationship, lacking the trust this requires, usually as a result of early developmental difficulties of their own (Erikson 1977). As for emotional defences, we all require these, indeed anyone whose defences are inadequate will pay an immense cost if working as a counsellor. However, as counsellors there are many times when we have to be able to reach across our own emotional defences in order to make the relational contact that counselling requires. An individual unable to do this will struggle in relationships generally, tending to seek to control inter-active situations rather than allowing the natural movement to take its own course. Some who are seeking such control may feel somewhat trapped within their own internal prison and consequently be drawn to work as a therapist because 'they believe, quite wrongly, that its practice will dispel the mists of their unperceptiveness' (Storr 1990: 183).

The third type of person, who has severe narcissistic tendencies, will also be unable to effectively engage in relationships in the manner required in therapeutic work. Narcissism takes its name from the Greek myth of Narcissus (Graves 1960) who became hopelessly lost in the reverie induced as he gazed at his own reflection. The term 'narcissistic' is used in somewhat confusing ways in psychotherapeutic literature (Pulver 1970). I am using the term to describe the person who exhibits particularly impenetrable defences that are constructed to protect a weak sense of personal identity and poor self-esteem (Schwartz-Salant 1982). In addition I would expect the narcissistic person to have a marked tendency to self-reference: to process experience with themselves, rather than others, as the principal if not the only reference point (Jacoby 1990).

We could add a fourth grouping of those who have personal mental health difficulties that they are not able to identify and contain. It is quite possible for people with recurring or chronic mental health difficulties, such as depression, anxiety states, eating disorders, addictions or the milder psychotic disorders to function as counsellors. In order to do so they must know when they are being affected by their condition and what the impact may be upon their work with clients. They must also be able to contain this impact effectively; not an easy undertaking. Those with mental health difficulties not able to meet these criteria are unlikely to be able to sustain themselves as effective counsellors.

When present to a substantial degree each of these forms of difficulty would inevitably restrict the ability of the counsellor to relate with sufficient empathy and warmth to instigate a working therapeutic relationship. In part it is the degree and depth of compulsion of the characteristics that determines whether or not the individual is capable of being an effective counsellor. Any who do have such difficulties to a prohibitive degree will probably lack an understanding that this is so, caught themselves within their internal defensive web. Thus it is important for the counselling profession to act responsibly in this regard: taking steps to identify and exclude those wishing to be counsellors who are not suited to the role. It is also important to recognise that working as a counsellor can exacerbate some of these tendencies and make the symptoms more profound. I shall return to this later in this chapter when I consider the counselling mask.

The second determinant of an individual's ability to contain emotional and psychological vulnerabilities sufficiently to be an effective counsellor is their degree of conscious awareness. In an interesting study Wosket (1990) used a factor analysis procedure upon responses to a questionnaire on counsellor motivation which was distributed to a number of trained counsellors or those with substantial experience. Although only a relatively small sample, twenty-four counsellors, responded, some of the differences are worthy of note. Topping the table of what counsellors considered to be their primary motivators were 'client growth' (mentioned sixteen times) and 'personal development of the counsellor' (fourteen). Halfway down the list came 'curiosity', 'calling', and 'influence of significant others' (eight) with 'stress' and 'need to be needed or succour others' (three) the least frequently found themes. This is a study of what this sample of counsellors believe to be their motivation for being in this work. We see that the personal development of the counsellor is recognised as a motivating factor almost as frequently as client growth. This is quite encouraging as it suggests a high degree of conscious awareness that counselling is a process in which both participants are looking for gain. This implies a healthy balance in recognising both altruistic and self-interest motivations. However, personal development is a somewhat benign general description and does not give a great deal of information as to how far down the road of self-awareness these practitioners have in fact travelled.

Such a study of conscious motivations sheds little light on the unconscious factors also present. In an intriguingly paradoxical proposition Street (1989) has suggested that one of the fascinations available to counsellors is the ever unfolding process of realising the different layers of motivation that bring us into this field. In the early years of being a counsellor a recognition of such factors as the desire to emulate those who have been helpful to us, the wish to help others, or a sense of calling may suffice. Gradually other, perhaps less palatable, factors start to be uncovered: the need to be needed, a perhaps slightly macabre curiosity that borders on voyeurism, an enjoyment of the sense of being important for our clients. It is as if we are ever identifying different significant factors and as each is recognised so it loses some of its potency, becomes less of a need or even demand, and we move on to a new layer of understanding ourselves. This is the process of exploring and coming to know aspects of our own shadow.

FORMING THE SHADOW

The foundations for the personal shadow are laid at an early age, although the manifestations often do not come to light until adulthood. As a child grows and develops the favourable aspects of their personality, the behaviours, qualities, skills, feelings and desires that are valued, are encouraged and will tend to be integrated into the consciously experienced sense of self. Usually a personal identity or sense of self forms, which is dominated by those aspects of the young person that are favoured by those with influence over them and by the social and cultural context within which they find themselves. Meanwhile the child also develops a shadow side into which they place and thereby repress those aspects of themselves that they learn are disliked or unacceptable to those who have influence upon them.

This process of splitting off aspects of personality may take place in an unobtrusive manner, but in some instances is born out of explicit, and at times dramatic, struggle. You may have witnessed scenes in these dramas that can take many weeks, months or even years to run their course. I recall observing the conflict between a two-year-old and his parents that seemed destined to result in shadow material being generated. The boy in question was quite slow in his speech development and on occasions his frustration erupted and he switched from looking somewhat bewildered into a rage of kicking and punching. His parents would intervene both to protect those on the receiving end of his attack and also to try to curb behaviour that manifestly caused them considerable discomfort and embarrassment. As a bystander with little emotional involvement in what was occurring it was easy to see that the child's violence was a result of his frustration in not being able to make himself understood. It is then but a short step to criticising the parents for focusing their attention on trying to control his behaviour rather than endeavouring to understand what the child was attempting to communicate prior to becoming so angry. However, when fists and feet are flying and the child is singularly unavailable to reasoning, the attempts of the parents to exert their authority upon the situation are easy to understand. While not having certain knowledge of what will result from this situation, it is an example of the type of interaction that can lead, over time, to the frustrated angry side to that child being suppressed and residing in his shadow. Then a seemingly satisfactory resolution occurs: the parents are greatly relieved that their little boy no longer has these tantrums and the child is rewarded by increased positive attention and reward. However, there is a psychological cost to such a split: it takes a certain amount of the child's psychic energy to contain the unexpressed emotion, energy that is not available for other purposes. This is reflected delightfully in the image Bly (1988) uses for the shadow, describing it as a long bag that we drag along and into which we stuff all the unwanted aspects of ourselves we encounter. This image offers a way of sensing the effect of having a shadow: it is hard work proceeding through life while constantly having to drag a heavy bag!

This description of the development of the child into adulthood is manifestly oversimplified, as is demonstrated by the clientele of any counsellor's consulting room. Were it an accurate and total description of the development process then we would all grow up with a positive, if distorted, view of ourselves in blissful unawareness of the contents of our shadow bag. In reality many people struggle to find anything about themselves that is likeable or acceptable. A more complete picture of the development of a person would need to take into account a range of other factors. These include significant life events, the psychological nature of the key figures in the person's life, the construction of the family (or other social grouping) in which the person grows up as well as the social and political events that have an impact. Depending upon your beliefs about how personality forms you may also want to take innate characteristics of the individual into account. However, this process of splitting during childhood development is an important facet of the process of a personality developing and forms one of the major sources of material within the personal shadow. As the personal shadow is formed so too the ego is also being created – the central organising function within the consciously experienced self. It is as well to avoid the danger of muddling the psychological function of ego with the somewhat more value-laden popular description of 'ego-tism'. This unfortunate term distorts the merely descriptive term of ego into a synonym for selfishness. Undoubtedly an over-inflated ego may lead the possessor to be somewhat selfish in attitude and action; however, a properly developed ego is essential for psychological health and is not to be spurned or devalued.

Accepting that the development of the shadow takes place within a complex environment, nevertheless, a process of division occurs within the personal psyche. Having reached adulthood each of us has an identity that may not be particularly well articulated but does provide us with some grasp of what it is to be 'me'. Meanwhile those other aspects of our psyche that do not fit our personal description of who 'I am' have been banished into our shadow side.

It is tempting to think of the psychological process of splitting, which results in the formation of a personal shadow, as an unfortunate phenomenon better avoided. In reality it would appear that it provides a very valuable resource to the developing psyche, enabling the maintenance of a sufficient degree of 'self-coherence' (Horowitz 1989) by providing a necessary means to sift through the range of experiences to which the individual is subject. Jacobs suggests that 'learning to integrate good and bad experiences' which 'is essential if we are to make realistic assessments of the relative merits and faults of ourselves, of others and of situations in which we find ourselves . . . is clearly a lifetime's task' (1986: 44). Accepting this time-scale then makes it apparent that it is beyond the psychological resources of the child or young person to deal with the ambivalence and conflicts with which life presents them so that the defence of repression that leads to splitting is a necessary and therefore valuable mechanism. Fairbairn (1940) goes as far as to suggest that splitting is a universal phenomenon at the deeper levels of the psyche, supporting this proposition through the interpretation that we all produce more than one figure to represent ourselves in dreams. This may be journeying further into deep psychology than some are prepared to travel; nevertheless, it does lend support to the suggestion that far from being an abnormal process made necessary by extremes of experience splitting is a helpful mechanism we probably all employ.

Having formulated the principle that splitting occurs and that it serves a valuable psychological function it seems appropriate to clarify what gets split off in this way. In the earlier example of the child it is the violent expression of a powerful emotional state that is the subject of parental disapproval. It is not possible to be certain whether the child will split off only the behaviour, i.e. violent aggression, or whether he will also banish to his shadow the emotional experience of anger and frustration that led to that violence. However, it is most likely that both the felt experience and its physical expression will become repressed, as the predominant tendency is that 'strong feeling is unconsciously tied to some physical act that we think should give expression to it' (Johnson 1993: 5). Therefore if the capacity to distinguish between the emotional experience itself and the manifestation of that emotion in a physical act is lacking then both must be put aside. In the consulting room I meet many clients who initially seem utterly out of touch (I use this tactile term deliberately) with any internal experience of some or all emotional states. There are varying degrees to this emotional numbness with the most extreme seemingly unaware of any subtlety of sensation. Others have an awareness of physical sensation that is a manifestation of emotional experience but lack the capacity to differentiate between degrees of emotional response and perhaps the vocabulary to articulate those emotions. It is no coincidence that much of the attention of humanistic therapeutic approaches (Rowan 1983) is concerned with assisting people to express emotions in a direct and often physical manner. In part this emphasis upon cathartic expression, which is ably positioned among intervention strategies by Heron (1990), grew out of the belief that the other principal therapeutic orientations were weak in this area. Psychoanalytical-oriented therapy tended to emphasise increased insight and behavioural approaches were primarily concerned with changing how the person acts. In both, increasing the capacity of the client to directly experience emotions seemed to be a secondary concern whereas 'the aim of most so called humanistic therapies is to heal the split between the ego itself and the body' (Wilber 1979: 12) with the term 'body' including the sensation function (Whitmont 1991), which is the channel through which we access emotion. The therapeutic field has shifted somewhat in recent decades and there is evidence of considerable cross fertilisation such that the traditional distinctions between the analytic, behavioural and humanistic schools are somewhat more blurred in the current practice of many therapists (Norcross and Grencavage 1989). Nevertheless, the emphasis given by many practitioners to enable clients to reconnect with their emotional experience is a measure of the number of people for whom this is a difficulty.

The manner in which powerful emotion and its expression can become repressed and thereby reside in the shadow will have considerable consequences. It is not possible to simply take one aspect of emotional experience, be it anger, sadness, delight, fear, hate, surprise, joy or whatever, isolate that emotion and determine to banish it from our experience. Rather, in the process of excluding a specific emotional state from our consciousness we restrict the effectiveness of the feeling function overall. Heron describes the relationship between emotion and feeling thus: 'Feeling is the ground of emotion. By our felt participation in a situation we appraise it as fulfilling or frustrating our present need and this engenders our emotional state' (1992: 23).

In restricting felt experience the capacity to engage with or participate in the situations within which we live becomes damaged. This results in an impairment of the capacity to be in relationship with others that in an extreme form leads to what is termed in psycho-pathological language as the schizoid position (Storr 1990). Thus it begins to become clear that the banishing of aspects of self to the shadow, while providing an essential self-protective function, can have far-reaching and costly consequences.

There is another element in what has become shadow material, for along with the emotional content and the linked behaviour there must also be a belief. The toddler repressing his violent impulses develops a belief that he is not an aggressive person. The belief is essential, as it is with this that the ego is able to build and maintain the barrier that keeps the shadow material firmly held in unconsciousness. However, this presents the individual with something of a dilemma because inevitably such a belief will be imbalanced: I am this sort of person not that sort of person. There are likely to be events in the person's life that call such a view into question, so if this process of splitting is to be effective the psyche needs a means of dealing with such situations.

To explore this further let us consider another example, that of Diane, whose story we shall pick up when she has reached her thirties. One of the primary characteristics contained in Diane's shadow is her desire to take charge in whatever she is involved in. She had, during her childhood years, opted to deny her tendency to take the lead in favour of gaining the acceptance and approval of her peers by offering a more compliant persona. She had gone on to start a promising career in librarianship and then to marry Andrew. Although she enjoyed her work she acquiesced to Andrew's wish to start a family, leaving her job at 27 when she discovered that she was pregnant. From that point Diane devoted herself to the home, their two delightful children, and supporting Andrew in his career. For a few years this worked well but gradually the psychological toll made its presence felt through increasing depression. At the point Diane entered therapy she had been diagnosed clinically depressed, was struggling to manage her family responsibilities and was fearful for her marriage. At the outset there are few clues for her therapist as to the causes of her condition and Diane herself has little insight, being preoccupied with the sense of hopelessness that pervades her experience.

The therapy makes little headway until Diane talks about a recent visit from her mother-in-law. For the first time she becomes really animated in the session, expressing outrage and fury at how bossy and interfering she finds her mother-in-law's behaviour. The therapist, delighted to see finally some spark of energy in Diane pursues this, eliciting examples of the offending relative's behaviour. However, the mother-in-law seems, to the therapist, to be behaving in a relatively inoffensive manner: proposing a baby-sitter so that she can take Diane and Andrew out for a meal, buying some clothes for the children and giving her opinion during a discussion on colour schemes for a room Diane wants to decorate. The therapist is struck by the apparent mismatch between these examples of the behaviour of the mother-in-law and the intensity of rage experienced by Diane – the emotional equation does not appear to balance. An inexperienced or cautious therapist might let such a clue pass, for to challenge this mismatch demands a degree of courage. It requires the therapist to stand by their assessment, judgement even, of the appropriate level of emotional response to these particular experiences.

In Diane's case her therapist did take this risk, proposing that the level of her felt response indicated that perhaps some unconscious force was at work. In this she was drawing on her knowledge of the theory of the defence mechanism of projection in which an aspect of ourselves is repressed, held unconscious, and then reacted to when perceived in others. The clue to there being a projection process at work lies in what Whitmont terms 'the emotional coloring' (1991: 60). In other words it is the very fact of there being a powerful affective response to the situation that confirms the therapist's suspicion that the shadow is literally making its presence felt. To enable Diane to start the process of owning the projected material takes sensitivity and compassion. This requires Diane to identify those aspects of her mother-in-law to which she reacts most powerfully and search out those same attributes within herself: attributes that Diane has gone to considerable lengths to deny for so long.

It is this mechanism of projection, this capacity developed by the psyche to maintain the distorted self-image that results from splitting off aspects of personality and rendering them seemingly invisible, which acts as a psychological and emotional pressure valve. For Diane, directing her anger towards her mother-in-law serves a number of functions simultaneously. It provides a means of releasing her pent-up frustration, it offers an opportunity to rationalise her belief that she is an accommodating compliant person and it also allows her to stay at the emotional level of anger thereby avoiding the pain that lurks beneath. We can imagine the internal dialogue, the conversation Diane would be having with herself: 'Well really! I would never behave like that, how selfish of her.' By focusing her anger and frustration onto another person Diane avoids the uncomfortable truth that she is angry and frustrated with her own circumstances and no longer wishes to play second fiddle while Andrew leads the orchestra. Indeed, by making her mother-in-law the object of her frustration she also confuses the psychological trail: it would be too close for comfort to direct her anger towards Andrew. Happily the mechanism of projection not only provides a safety valve, when recognised it also provides a powerful clue as to what else is taking place at an unconscious level.

THE COUNSELLOR'S PERSONAL SHADOW

Each of us forms a personal shadow as part of our psychological development and so, inevitably, we bring this with us into our work as counsellors. I want to emphasise the importance of keeping this within our awareness. Even when we know intellectually that we have a shadow and have experience of manifestations of our own personal shadow we remain vulnerable to the possibility of denial. It is not surprising that such a temptation exists, for it is the very essence of ego to seek ways to confirm its own sense of being in control. One of the strengths of the concept of shadow as a description of unconscious aspects of ourselves lies in the imagery it creates. I have already referred to its connotations of 'darkness' and 'otherness' but it also possesses the attribute of 'constancy'. By this I mean that in the physical realm we know that wherever we are, provided there is some illumination, we cast a shadow. I find this a useful counter to my tendency, which I feel sure I share with others, to conveniently 'forget' about my unconscious at times when it is uncomfortable to acknowledge its existence.

As counsellors our personal shadow will be present when we are in the counselling arena just as it is present in every other aspect of our lives. It will have its own agenda and there are likely to be items on this agenda that run contrary to the best interests of clients. It is important, therefore, that we seek to uncover our shadow agenda and neutralise its harmful potential. At any given point on this journey of self-discovery those needs that are still buried in unawareness remain free to influence and affect our therapeutic work. This process of discovering our shadow is as much for ourselves as for our clients. There seems little doubt that a considerable proportion of those of us who enter the world of counselling do so as a means of tackling our own inadequacies and difficulties: seeking our own healing (Goldberg 1986). Being a counsellor confronts us with our shadow and in doing so opens up the possibility of renewed contact with our inner wisdom and resources that have either been lost or previously lain dormant.

THE COUNSELLING MASK

Uncovering the effect of our personal shadow on our practice is made more complex by the counsellor persona[2] we inevitably create. This persona, or mask, is constructed as we train, built from the skills themselves, modelled upon the counsellors, supervisors and trainers we seek to emulate and shaped by the necessary boundaries of the role. We all have other persona that we adopt in a fairly routine manner according to the different situations we are in. I know that I am different with my family to the way I am at work. I also differ in how I behave towards my immediate colleagues and among others in the institution with whom I have more formal and distant and at times politically complex relationships. I behave differently with those intimate friends I have known for many years to the way I behave in more recently formed friendships. As Samuels puts it: 'Over a lifetime, many personas will be worn and several may be combined at any one moment' (1985: 107). The creation of a counsellor persona has parallels with the development of ego, i.e. desired attributes being emphasised and undesirable ones being discarded, although it is very much a shallow echo as it takes place with a considerable degree of consciousness. I know, for instance, that for myself in my counsellor persona I am receptive and reflective, listening carefully to what is being said. I seldom speak of myself or my own circumstances and am quite deliberate in what I do say. I am particularly alert to how my words might be heard and pay a lot of attention to my thoughts and feelings. I am also fairly deliberate in the way I greet and take my leave of clients. This is quite different to how I am in other settings where I can be quite talkative and not always particularly sensitive to the effect I have on others. In the early stages the counsellor is endeavouring to find a way to don this role, this new way of being when working with a client.

Eckler-Hart (1987) has described this process as the development of the therapist's 'false self', which refers back to the work of Winnicott.[3] This false self is a necessary attribute of the therapist for it contains those aspects of the personhood of the practitioner that are inappropriate to the therapeutic role and it protects the vulnerability of the therapist from undue exposure. Without it therefore both client and counsellor are overly vulnerable in the counselling relationship and this is particularly the case in the beginnings of counselling practice. Yet the term will inevitably leave us all a little uncomfortable for to take on a mantle of 'false-ness' would appear antipathetic to the genuineness or real relationship that is so fundamental to effective therapeutic work.

This persona will fit with varying degrees of ease for different practitioners and the quality of fit is also likely to vary at different stages of each individual's career. At best we are able to take on this counsellor persona and mould it in a manner that fits our personality and natural style and do so with sufficient flexibility that the role can readily adjust as we continue to mature (McConnaughy 1987). This is the ideal and those who realise it will be able to journey through life as a person and counsellor without undue friction between the two. However, I would anticipate that the majority of counsellors will go through periods when this progression is not so painless. Indeed periods of discomfort, of poor fit between role and person, are virtually inevitable as we develop and change. For some these will be but brief interludes in an otherwise smooth passage and may be nothing more than the distress that often marks a passage of personal growth. For others such discomfort may be the herald of serious crises that, ultimately, can lead to the person ceasing to practise as a counsellor.

In addition to temporary periods of discomfort it is also feasible that donning the role of counsellor will result in harm to the person: the individual suffering emotional or psychological damage. This is an alarming idea to contemplate but nevertheless it needs to be acknowledged that this can, and on occasions does, occur. When this does happen the person is disabled by the experience of being a counsellor, suffering difficulties that may be irrecoverable. Both these possibilities, transitory periods of discomfort and more permanent harm to the person who is counsellor, can be considered within the framework of the personal ego, shadow and counselling persona.

In psychological structure terms I position the counsellor persona largely within the ego. However, as illustrated in Figure 2, we can anticipate overlaps between the counselling persona we adopt and our personal shadow. It is in these areas of overlap that some of our unconscious motivations for being counsellors will be found, and it is in such an area of overlap that my desire for contained intimacy exists: it is a legitimate part of the counselling persona but also part of my personal shadow. Therefore I have to be careful about this desire of mine because the intimacy offered in the counselling relationship can develop an addictive quality. At times the interaction between counsellor and client has an intensity of feeling and of mutual

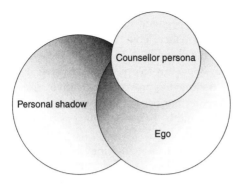

Figure 2 Ego, personal shadow and counsellor persona

vulnerability (Miller and Baldwin 1987) that is uncommon across the relationship spectrum. Yet this takes place in a context in which little information about the counsellor is known to the client, whereas the counsellor usually has a great deal of detailed information about the client and an implicit licence to elicit more. It is not difficult to imagine that for some counsellors this may be a very attractive setting in which to seek the satisfaction of certain forms of intimacy need. There is, rightfully, considerable attention given to when these needs are manifestly exploitative of the client (Pope 1990; Strasburger *et al.* 1992), but the dangers to the counsellor are less well debated.

For those practitioners whose personal relationships are problematic or unsatisfactory there is a particular risk that the intimacy of the consulting room becomes a substitute or replacement. If unchecked this may lead to further damage to other relationships and can result in a form of addiction in which the practitioner is left feeling fully in contact with others only when counselling. This is clearly an unsatisfactory state of affairs and may be the precursor to exploitation of clients alongside increasing personal difficulties for the counsellor. For some it may be a temporary stage that they pass through, finding a new depth of intimacy and self-awareness first in the therapeutic relationship. The balance then needs to be found in more deeply satisfying personal relationships in order that this does not become a more permanent state (Raskin 1978).

This is one example of a general phenomenon that can occur: resonance[4] between the personal shadow of the counsellor and the role. Resonance in this context describes the process whereby some aspect of the personal shadow of the practitioner is amplified by some part of the role. A second example is someone who has a disposition towards passivity becoming increasingly so as they spend time in the role of counsellor. Being a counsellor is not a passive activity by any means; however, the attentiveness and stillness required in the role have sufficient similarity to passivity to set up a resonance. Thus the individual with a propensity for passivity is in danger that this will increasingly take hold as they practise as a counsellor. If they find a way to become less passive, more active, then it could be said that the role has provoked a creative crisis that has led to growth. However, should their passivity increase until their functionality deteriorates then this would be better described as the counsellor having come to harm.

Another area where there is almost inevitable resonance for us all relates to our narcissistic tendencies. I have already suggested that those with severe narcissistic difficulties are unsuited to being a counsellor, but before dismissing these characteristics as grossly antipathetic to the therapeutic endeavour we should pause and think again. In a mild form they are not dissimilar to important characteristics that, it can be argued, therapeutic practitioners do well to cultivate in order to do the work. An effective practitioner needs a degree of emotional resilience, a capacity to protect against the emotional attacks that clients will on occasions launch. Alongside this it is recognised that an effective therapist will be well able to deal with and process their emotional experience, will have cultivated the tendency to be almost constantly aware of what they feel in response to the client.

This is not to suggest that a person with a strongly embedded narcissistic character will make a good therapist, far from it. Such a person is likely to shy away from contact with the client, have poor empathic capacity and defend against rather than work with any hostility expressed by the client. In addition they may well unwittingly encourage idealised transference from the client that will be used to feed a sense of personal grandiosity (as a compensation for a sense of inferiority) with little investment in working through this material in the interests of the client. Such a person is definitely not to be welcomed into the consulting room! What needs to be recognised is not only that people with narcissistic tendencies may be drawn to this field but more significantly for all practitioners any latent narcissistic tendencies within each one of us may be drawn out and amplified by being in this work. We will all have to find a way through these particular dangers for we each have to engage our narcissistic selves in order to develop our reflective capacities.

The narcissistic dangers are opened up by the need for the counsellor to look inside. The second aspect of reflection is developing an intellectual understanding, a set of theoretical constructs with which to make sense of the therapeutic process. This generates other dangers for the counsellor that are encapsulated in the possibility of being seduced into the intellectual realm. This can draw the counsellor away from their compassionate responses and encourage an objectifying of the client: seeing the client as a particular sort of 'problem' or an 'interesting case'. It is a particular danger for those counsellors who are seeking to find certainty: an additional resource with which to supplement their defences against the anxieties of everyday life (Storr 1990). If these are solidly constructed defences then it can be argued that such a person has already made a decision that renders them unsuited to therapeutic work: they have chosen in favour of psychological defence rather than the uncertainty that comes with growth. It is unlikely that such an individual will honestly engage with a client, be willing to be emotionally present with this other person in the manner that effective therapeutic encounter requires (Shainberg 1983). They would fall into the category, described earlier, of those who are so 'compulsively emotionally defended' that they are unsuited to being a counsellor.

Many will not be so compulsively defended but may be seduced for a while into this form of intellectual defence and in so doing may be unwittingly cruel or persecutory towards clients. When counsellors first develop the capacity to view others from a perspective of psychological mindedness (Farber 1983) a great sense of clarity and understanding can result. It is tempting to want to share what this perception brings, sometimes with insufficient regard to the client's capacity to hear and utilise what is being said.

There is another form of resonance that can occur when an aspect of the role of counsellor interacts with an opposing characteristic within the counsellor's personal shadow. Let us consider a counsellor who has an innate tendency towards impatience. Sitting quietly and attentively and allowing the direction to emerge from the client would gradually impart increasing pressure upon the shadow desire within the counsellor for action or movement. This may well culminate in the counsellor acting in a counter-therapeutic manner, expressing their impatience and leaving the client feeling criticised or pressured. In this instance the patience demanded by the role is in 'counter-resonance' with the impatient aspect of the personal shadow of the counsellor. In general terms we can anticipate counter-resonance with those personal attributes that run contrary to the qualities and skills of the counsellor. In contrast, resonance occurs with characteristics that can be thought of as complementing those same counselling qualities and skills.

Resonance or counter-resonance is likely to take some time to emerge as there is usually a honeymoon period when a counsellor starts to practise, it is all very new and exciting and probably the culmination of many months or years of training and preparation. This will carry the new counsellor forward for some time, almost breathless as they watch clients move forward and make changes. In part the honeymoon is a consequence of newness, but it is also a period when the majority of counsellors work with relatively few clients. Thus if internal pressure is to build up within the psyche of the counsellor as a result of the tension between the role and the personal shadow this will take longer when seeing a small number of clients. As the months go by, the counsellor's caseload increases and the initial euphoria wears off, then the conditions are more favourable for shadow material that is resonating or counter-resonating with the role to come to light.

Any aspect of the role might have this effect so we shall just consider, as a typical example, the aspect of the role that can best be described as having a compassionate attitude. This is an important attribute, being fundamental to the quality of therapeutic relationship between counsellor and client. If the person who is the counsellor also has a shadow dis-passionate side this is not so readily welcomed in the consulting room. Dispassion can be thought of as cold and lifeless: distant and disengaged, unwilling to be involved and lacking depth of feeling for the other person. At worst this can move towards the cruel and sadistic, taking pleasure in inflicting punishment and pain, in causing suffering rather than alleviating it. Given that most of us will contain a mixture of compassionate and dispassionate tendencies, moving into the role of counsellor will set up a potential conflict within us. One solution to this conflict is to emphasise the seemingly desirable compassion and push to one side its corollary. Thus the dispassionate side to our nature may be pushed further into the dimness of our personal shadow. For a while this will probably work really well as we throw ourselves enthusiastically into the task. If this enthusiasm is based upon denial of our dispassionate side then this must no longer be sustainable at some point. The dispassionate aspect will demand expression in one forum or another. It may be displaced so that we find ourselves very compassionate and committed to our clients but cut off and disinterested in our personal relationships. It may start to leak back into our counselling work: being sharp with one client, losing interest in where the work is going with another. I do not offer this as a prescription of what must occur but rather as a description for what may be experienced.

In reality dispassion does have a significant and appropriate place in our counselling, when balanced by compassion. It is the source of the un-compromising presumption we draw on when we confront (Heron 1990) or when we refuse to offer inappropriate sympathy or reassurance. I recollect coming in to a lunchtime staff meeting in a residential therapeutic com-munity for teenagers to find those who had been working that morning drained and demoralised. They had been struggling hard to contain one particularly distressed and damaged teenager but she had cut her arms quite badly and had been admitted to the casualty department in the local hospital with the inevitable psychiatric assessment and risk of compulsory admission. There was a sense of defeat and consequently little energy with which to meet the other dozen or so agitated residents. Gradually the locus of the conversation shifted away from the very real concern for this particular resident into what an obnoxious bunch of people it was our sorry lot to deal with. After a while a social work student who was on placement with the community at the time could take no more of this and started accusing us of not acting professionally. It was pointed out to him that while the content of what was being said might be judged unprofessional the increased energy which was palpable in the room was a professional necessity in order to fulfil our responsibilities to the young people in our charge. It was true that what was being said was far from being compassionate or concerned but the increased energy could not be denied. Many interpretations can be placed on such an incident but in my view it was an example of a healthy expression of the shadow side of compassion. It seemed as if the workers had exhausted themselves with their concern for this young woman and it was only by getting in touch with harder, dispassionate, more aggressive feelings towards the residents in the community that they could re-energise themselves.

The dispassionate side also has an important part to play in the creation and maintenance of therapeutic boundaries. There will be occasions when the palpable neediness of the client puts pressure on those boundaries and if we allow our emotional response to dictate we may act in ways which, in the cooler light of dispassionate reflection, we know are likely to be counterproductive. I had an example of this with a client who needed to negotiate extra time for academic work that had not been done because of distressing personal circumstances. They felt embarrassed and were dreading facing their academic supervisor, even though they had a good relationship with this person. I felt harsh when I refused their direct plea that I contact the supervisor on their behalf and the client was clearly disappointed and angry with me. Yet a week later they expressed their gratitude, the meeting with the supervisor had gone very well and encouraged the client to make a start on the essays. There might be circumstances when I would have acted differently but such a decision is best based on therapeutic criteria, not emotional responses.

I do not believe that the resting place for the pendulum is really at the compassionate end of the swing, it belongs in the middle where compassion and dispassion meet, where both are present. However, when we embark on the path of becoming a counsellor it is important that we take on the mantle of compassion, that we aspire to this seemingly laudable quality. In doing so it is to be hoped that we create a container for some of the potential for cruelty and desire to inflict pain that we also may bring with us. Those who train as counsellors later in life may well already have done the psychological work required for this container to be unnecessary. It is the work of learning how to recognise and acknowledge the desire to hurt when it arises and then to contain the desire so it does not become manifest in action. We need to be mindful that in the counselling context where the client is particularly vulnerable it is quite possible to be hurtful without blatant animosity. A mildly sarcastic or cutting comment that may well go virtually unnoticed in a social setting can cause considerable pain. Consequently, we have to be quite sophisticated in detecting the ways we may inadvertently act out our desire to inflict hurt. Once we have consciously accepted that we have a capacity to do harm within us then I believe it becomes much less likely that we shall in fact do so. When we deny this possibility to ourselves we are much more vulnerable to it catching us unawares. For those counsellors who have not as yet confronted their potential to do damage it is probably in everyone's interests that they adopt a position of compassion even though there may be an element of distortion in so doing.

I have suggested that the existence of the counsellor persona complicates the task of shadow discovery. At the same time it serves as a protective mechanism for the client because it helps to contain the counsellor within their role. To give a simple illustration my more talkative and insensitive aspects are not part of my counsellor persona and so seldom intrude upon my counselling work. From time to time I might think that I am saying more than usual and have learnt to check whether I am being appropriate to my role as a counsellor for the particular client I am with.

THE MALEVOLENT COUNSELLOR

There is a considerable body of evidence that some counsellors do act in ways that are perceived as harming clients. Perhaps best known are the examples of counsellors seeking sexual satisfaction, sometimes at enormous cost to clients. Studies have shown varying levels of sexual interaction between clients and therapists. Pope *et al.* (1979) quote 12 per cent of male therapists and 3 per cent of female therapists engaging in sexual contact with clients. Similarly amongst a group of psychologists practising psychotherapy Holroyd and Brodsky (1977) found that 11 per cent of males and 2 per cent of females reported erotic contact while 5.5 per cent of males and 0.6 per cent of females acknowledged having had sexual intercourse with a client while therapy was in progress. The range of sexual contact from subtle arousing touch through to full penetrative intercourse is substantial and the degree of impact upon individual clients also varies widely. Russell (1993) has discussed these and other issues of sexual inter-action between clients and counsellors in considerable depth. What must be concluded from the various studies is that a significant number of clients experience themselves to be hurt or damaged through sexual contact with their counsellor or therapist.

There are also instances reported where the boundaries of confidentiality are not treated with due respect. Welfel and Lipsitz (1984) suggest that this is an area of considerable confusion among practitioners. In my own research into aspects of counselling practise (Page 1992) I found significant inconsistencies between the information given to clients regarding confi-dentiality and likely reasons for client information being passed on to a third party. In a sample of fifty-six counsellors from across the UK (of which forty-eight held some form of professional accreditation) fourteen stated to clients that confidentiality was absolute and yet, of those, five offered one or more sets of circumstances in which they would break confi-dentiality. Only twenty of the fifty-six told clients that they might discuss their counselling in supervision although all respondents were members of the British Association for Counselling and therefore required to receive regular supervision of their therapeutic work. The trend throughout was that clients were told about possible breaches with significantly less frequency than the counsellors indicated that they were willing to breach confidentiality. Yet the findings of Jagim *et al.* (1978) indicate that clients anticipate complete confidentiality. Given this, in my view the respon-sibility of counsellors to proffer information as to the conditions in which confidentiality might not be maintained is unequivocal.

These represent two of the most commonly recognised areas of counsellor behaviour that are likely to result in significant harm to the client. Others include counsellors working beyond their competence, financial or emo-tional exploitation, not adhering to contractual agreements, improper use of techniques and acting in ways that undermine client autonomy. Despite the undeniable evidence that counsellors do harm clients I have not, as yet, met a counsellor who I believe has deliberately set out to do so. I have come across a number of counsellors who have acted in ways that I consider to be seriously damaging to their clients. However, in each instance I have come to the conclusion that they have retained a sincere, although in my judgement highly misguided, view that they are working to the benefit of their clients.

It is difficult to imagine an individual deliberately seeking to become a counsellor for the express purpose of exploiting, mistreating or harming clients in some way. It does, nevertheless, remain conceivable that some-one could consciously enter counselling in order to create an opportunity to act out their malevolent intentions. It would be foolishly naive to deny this possibility but, in my view, it is unnecessarily suspicious to anticipate this to have more than a very rare incidence.

2   Development of the counsellor and the incorporation of shadow

It is axiomatic to counsellors that human beings are involved in a continuing process of development and change. As Rogers put it: 'Whether one calls it a growth tendency, a drive towards self-actualisation, or a forward moving directional tendency, it is the mainspring of life, and is, in the last analysis, the tendency upon which all psychotherapy is based' (1967: 35). This need not be a naive or unduly optimistic hope, although at worst it can be converted into that, but rather should be grounded in the range of experiences we have throughout our lives. It can embrace the reality that at times we are concerned with how to find a way to accept events or changes in ourselves and our lives that we view in very negative terms. The losses, grief, frustrations and disappointments that we all face as our lives progress do provide opportunities for increasing maturity and wisdom. This is a very different form of growth to the exciting, sometimes euphoric experience of finding great joy in unlocking our hitherto unfulfilled potential. In my view a comprehensive understanding of development accommodates both these ends of the spectrum and the various shades between. Jung says something very similar to Rogers when he writes:

> I must however pay attention to the psychological fact that, so far as we can make out, *individuation* is a natural phenomenon, and in a way an inescapable goal, that we have reason to call *good for us*, because it liberates us from the otherwise insoluble conflict of opposites (at least to a noticeable degree). It is not invented by man, but Nature herself produces its archetypal image.
>
> (1977: 164; original italics)

As counsellors we are often attempting to facilitate this process in our clients, assisting them to remove the blockages or find ways to hold together the seemingly contradictory aspects of themselves so that their development can continue. For ourselves we are concerned with our growth as people and also as practitioners. Wilkins (1997) points out that it is difficult to separate out the personal and professional aspects of development for a counsellor as they are so inexorably intertwined. However, he does go on to describe the professional aspect as 'that area which addresses the extension of skills and knowledge' (ibid.: 6). In contrast his definition of personal development includes the statement that 'Personal growth is the process of attending to our needs in such a way as to increase our ability to be with our clients' (ibid.: 9).

One of the earliest models specific to the development of the counsellor or therapist is that offered by Hogan (1964). He describes four levels of development through which therapists progress. In the first they are insecure, dependent, lacking insight, highly motivated, tend to rely on a limited therapeutic approach and learn by imitating more experienced practitioners. In level two there is tendency to swing between over-confidence and feeling overwhelmed, movement between autonomy and dependence and fluctuation of motivation for the work. In level three the practitioner is more confident and has greater insight into their motivation for choosing this field and there is a more stable sense of functioning autonomously. In the fourth level the therapist has a sense of personal and professional autonomy with increased confidence in themselves as a practitioner. There is an underlying sense of security and a willingness to confront difficulties as they emerge. This model forms the basis of the well-known integrated development model of Stoltenberg and Delworth (1987), written from a supervision perspective, which has been summarised elsewhere (Page and Wosket 1994).

These and the other models that abound – for example Blocher (1983), Grater (1985) and Hess (1987) – provide useful frameworks for conceptualising the movement from novice through to proficient practitioner. However, this is only the first part of the professional life of a counsellor as most of us go on to many years of further practice. If we are to be fresh in our attitude to the work then our development must continue. Indeed we might take this a step further and allow the possibility that the continuing development of the counsellor is in itself a necessary ingredient in the facilitation of the client's development.

A more recent model derived directly from research conducted with the participation of one hundred counselling practitioners across the range of experience from beginners to those with twenty-five years or more in the field is presented by Skovolt and Rønnestad (1995). This model offers a comprehensive framework for considering the development of a counsellor throughout their whole career. The authors break each of their eight stages down into seven elements: central task; predominant affect;

predominant source of influence; role and working style; conceptual ideas; learning process and measures of effectiveness and satisfaction. Table 1 is a brief summary of this model in which the training terms 'graduate' school and 'internship' have been converted into the approximate UK equivalents of certificate/diploma training and immediate post-qualification practice. As it is in summary form it can be read to imply a greater degree of certainty than I think the authors originally intended; their more thorough description considers in detail the common themes that emerged in their research. This model includes elements of both the professional and the personal development of the counsellor. It is thorough and when I reflect upon my own experience and the development I observe in colleagues and supervisees this model fits well. However, it focuses more on the manifestations of development than the process by which it occurs. In contrast the notion of shadow can be used to look more directly at how the counsellor develops: how we come to know ourselves to a depth that allows authenticity in the counselling relationship which is genuine and facilitative of therapeutic work.

DEVELOPMENT AND THE SHADOW

Bly (1988), writing for the general reader, describes a five-part process of creating and then reclaiming the personal shadow. The first is exiling; the process of creating a shadow as the individual grows. The second stage starts when the projections on to others start to rattle as they become a little less certain or believable. The third Bly describes as the call upon moral intelligence to repair the rattle, a defensive response intended to restore the previous status quo. The fourth he associates with the sensation of 'diminishment' (ibid.: 36) when the person starts to recognise that many aspects of themselves have been discarded. As Jung puts it: 'Many – far too many – aspects of life that should also have been experienced lie in the lumber-room among dusty memories: but sometimes, too, they are glowing coals under grey ashes' (1969: 772). Bly's fifth stage is retrieval, when some of these 'glowing coals' are encouraged to burn again.

In considering the reclamation of the personal shadow as a developmental process, the question arises as to at what point in our lives we are ready to embark on this task. Jung (1969) used the image of the sun as it moves from dawn to dusk as a metaphor for the human life span, which he divided into four main stages. Childhood, or dawn, is largely driven by instinct as consciousness emerges. This period is characterised by a lack of internal conflict: external conflicts between the child and their environment may abound but there remains a singularity of internal

Table 1 A summary of the evolutionary stages presented by Skovolt and
Rønnestad (1995)

---

1 *Conventional*
The untrained person who tries to help others in a counselling-type manner.
They use what they naturally know and take up a role as sympathetic friend.
Drawing on their personal experience they apply common sense, learn through experience in the role and tend not to be particularly concerned to measure their effectiveness.

2 *Transition to professional training*
At this stage the person is starting out on training (typically certificate level) so is absorbing information from a variety of sources. They tend to be enthusiastic yet insecure, often feeling overwhelmed in their attempts to process all the new information and perspectives they are becoming exposed to. Typically the person is somewhat uncertain in their role as they try to combine theory with practice. Hungry for ideas and techniques, they are introspective and look for visible client improvement and feedback from a supervisor as means of evaluating their effectiveness.

3 *Imitation of experts*
At this stage the individual is moving through training (typically at diploma/ advanced diploma level) and endeavours to imitate experts in their counselling practice. Tending to shift from bewilderment to calm as an inflexible mastery of basic skills takes place. They respond to a range of influences: supervisors, clients, theory, research and their environment. Seeking out conceptual ideas and techniques they learn primarily through imitation, introspection and consideration. They evaluate their effectiveness through client feedback and responses from supervisor.

4 *Conditional autonomy*
This is the practitioner in their first 2 years post-qualification. Typically confidence fluctuates, they respond to multiple influences and have a fairly rigid sense of their role and style of work. By this stage the practitioner has a good understanding of the concepts and ideas of their therapeutic orientation. They continue to learn through selective imitation, introspection and thoughtful consideration. They are becoming more sophisticated in interpreting feedback from clients and supervisor.

5 *Exploration*
This is the period of 2–5 years post-qualification practice when the counsellor starts to explore beyond what they have been taught. They typically shift between confidence and anxiety, drawing on a range of influences including work settings and themselves as a professional. They are starting to modify the style taken on from others and reject some of the previously accepted conceptual ideas. More reflective and realistic in measuring their own effectiveness.

6 *Integration*
Between 5 and 10 years post-qualification, the counsellor is starting to develop authenticity and an increasing sense of satisfaction and hope. More able to recognise themselves as an experienced professional and moving between the original rigid role taken on from others and a looser internal style. Developing their own

conceptual system which integrates the ideas of others with their own, learning through a range of methods. They have internalised measures of effectiveness that are applied with increasing realism.

7 Individuation
From 10 to 30 years post-qualification, the practitioner has deepening authenticity while their predominant feeling about their work is both satisfaction and distress. The main influence upon them is accumulated wisdom from experience. Earlier sources internalised and have a sense of self as a professional elder. Increasingly themselves within appropriate professional boundaries. Concepts are individual and personalised, learning methods vary and evaluation is internal and realistic.

8 Integrity
From 30 years post-qualification onwards. The practitioner is facing the prospect of retirement with the primary feeling of acceptance. Influenced mainly by their internalised wisdom and in the role act very much as themselves. Concepts used are highly individual and integrated, learning methods vary greatly and evaluation is very much internal and realistic.

---

psychic experience. The second stage, which Jung calls 'youth', runs from puberty through to the middle years of 35–40 (from early morning through to midday). This is the time when the person establishes a place in the world through the work they do and the relationships they form. The focus is therefore primarily external and psychological accommodations and compromises may be made, in response to the emerging conflicts between different internal desires, in order to maintain the necessary equilibrium to achieve these external tasks. In this process important potentials within the person may be discarded and the personality consequently diminished.

At noon, or middle age, the sun reaches its zenith and a turning point occurs which Jung characterised as a looking inward. Those discarded aspects of self may be re-examined and some will go on to have an increasing influence upon the way the person lives. The shadow starts to emerge, as the person looks to their inner life more, less taken up by the demands of the external world. Many resist this process for a decade or longer, preferring the seeming stability and certainty offered by rigid beliefs and values. The fourth stage, old age or the evening of life, is very much influenced by how life has been lived. If satisfied then a quiet reflective old age is possible, but if frustrated and resentful then moving towards death is likely to be highly problematic.

Accepting this perspective would indicate that it will be in the middle years, from 35 onwards, that major work to reclaim the shadow starts to occur. There is a caveat to this given that Jung was writing in the 1930s and there has been a great deal of focus on increasing awareness and consciousness since then. My own view is that it is rather more a matter of psychological than chronological maturity that dictates the time-scale. I have worked with people in their late twenties and early thirties who seem to me to be involved in this task of shadow reclamation. My personal experience has been of my shadow making its presence most dramatically apparent in my early thirties although at the time of writing, a decade later, I recognise that there are elements of the main aspects of what emerged then that still remain accommodated rather than resolved. Counselling is likely to attract people who are naturally inward looking so that the personal exploration will start earlier than might be anticipated within the population as a whole. For all this it remains my view that few of us reach the psychological maturity to really begin addressing our shadow until our thirties. My impression is that in recent years, perhaps because counselling is becoming a more established profession, there has been an increasing number of young adults entering training with the intention of making counselling their first career. If this is indeed the case then it is particularly important that such counsellors are aware of their current level of development and the implications for the depth of therapeutic work they are ready to engage in.

A NEW FRAMEWORK

The model I will use to give some structure to the process of shadow creation and subsequent incorporation has six stages. This builds upon and also differs to some extent from Bly's (see p. 31) and I shall apply it specifically to the situation of the practising counsellor. As with any developmental model this is a general map and will not always accurately apply to the particular individual. Because it is a stage model applied to what might more precisely be thought of as a continuous process the boundaries between one stage and the next are sometimes quite blurred in reality. Also given that the shadow comprises a collection of distinct psychological elements it is probable that at any given time each of us will be at different stages with different aspects of our personal shadow. It is very important to be clear that this framework is not intended to be a model of the development of a counsellor. It is specifically a model for the shadow reclamation process that I anticipate any counsellor committed to their work will be involved in, although some may not describe it in these terms. The model is represented in Figure 3.

In producing this figure I have deliberately left each element in a some-what suspended state with no direct linkage to any other. This is intended to reflect the way we move in and out of consciousness of our relationship with our shadow: the shifting spotlight of awareness. It has been pointed

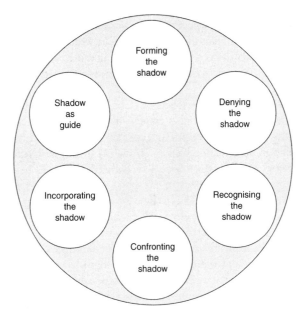

Figure 3 Evolutionary stages of shadow incorporation

out to me that there is a degree of similarity between the stages represented in this framework and the process of coming to terms with our own death. Kübler-Ross (1970) described five parts to this: denial and isolation; anger; bargaining; depression; and acceptance. On reflection this is not surprising as the shift from denial towards a greater acceptance of our shadow does involve a form of psychological death. It is the death of one construction of ourselves that is necessary in order that another can come into being.

Each of the six stages in the framework is the subject of a chapter, the first was addressed in Chapter 1 and stages two–six are considered in Chapters 3–7. At this point I want to summarise each one and then go on to look briefly at the relationship between the various stages.

Forming the shadow

The personal shadow is the main component in the counsellor's shadow and will have been established as the person, who later becomes a counsellor, grows into adulthood. It is also conceivable for new elements of shadow to be created as an adult, in particular when we take on the counsellor persona we may confine one or more aspects of ourselves to our shadow that have previously been consciously manifest. I now realise that

I 'lost' some of my sense of fun and mischief when I became involved in therapeutic work and I suspect that this was something to do with the sense of enormity of what I was undertaking. The re-emergence of this aspect of me in recent years has coincided with feeling more relaxed and at ease in my work with a greater sense of the ordinariness as well as privilege of being a counsellor.

I believe that this experience of mine is reasonably typical of what occurs when shadow material is created by taking on the counsellor role. It is as if a part of me became unconscious and largely unexpressed for a while but gradually came back of its own volition, with some conscious encouragement on my part once I recognised what was happening. My mischievousness is an aspect of my personality that does not easily fit into the counsellor role and has to be utilised with sensitivity if I am not to unwittingly undermine or belittle clients. Nevertheless, it is a significant part of who I am and therefore belongs within my genuine presence as a counsellor. There are many aspects of who counsellors may be as people that do not readily fit the role and we may banish some of these from all aspects of our lives until we have the confidence, born out of experience, to find ways to allow them into the therapeutic field.

Denying the shadow

Having been formed the psyche has considerable investment in maintaining the shadow within the unconscious. We all tend to employ the psychological mechanisms of denial and repression to achieve this. These mechanisms enable the split between the shadow and the ego to continue so that we can go about the important tasks the ego has to perform unencumbered by too much psychological ambiguity or complexity.

Practitioners who are at this stage are often over-identified with the counselling persona: the professional equivalent of the personal ego. This too serves an important function, as this period serves to embed the counsellor in their task. Our understanding of the counselling process may be somewhat simplistic at this point but that in itself can assist in providing a sound foundation upon which more complex understanding and more flexible practice can be built in the future.

While the shadow is being denied it is appropriate to be wary for it has the potential to be destructive without that necessarily being recognised by the counsellor. The clear boundaries and rigorous monitoring that are the hallmarks of good practice help to contain the shadow until such time as it can be recognised and, eventually, utilised in a constructive manner.

Recognising the shadow

As we move into this stage it starts to become possible to see and recognise the shadow at times although it still remains an enemy to be treated warily – to be managed and kept away from work with clients. It is difficult to know when it will become possible for each one of us to recognise our personal shadow in this way. In all probability there will be a number of occasions when the same unconscious motivation dictates actions, when the shadow can be recognised to be at work if we have the capacity to see this to be the case. As has already been suggested we are only ready to perceive our own shadow at work when we are sufficiently psychologically mature. When an aspect of the shadow is fully perceived for the first time, our conscious sense of ourselves, our self-image, receives a very considerable blow. No longer can we hold on to the particular view we have built of ourselves and we must have the psychological capacity to deal with this knowledge. Think back to the example in Chapter 1 of the violent frustrated two-year-old child and imagine how as an adult he might be deeply afraid of starting to express his anger and frustration. He has an emotional memory of being completely engulfed in his angry feelings so is likely to be understandably frightened to unleash such feelings. In reality the emotional intensity of the two-year-old is now tempered by many years of self-restraint so that the fear of his own potential destructive capacity is highly disproportionate. Certainly in the relatively controlled environment of the consulting room or group room such contacting with feelings that have been suppressed for many years is, in my experience, manageable and not as overwhelming as feared. This is not necessarily the case when such feelings are enacted without conscious recognition of their source, for then the feelings have at their disposal the strength and knowledge of the mature adult with which to reek havoc. However, recognition is unlikely to occur until the individual is ready to take this risk for themselves, or is no longer willing to pay the price of keeping their shadow unconscious.

Confronting the shadow

It appears that there are two forces at work when the shadow starts to emerge into the light of day. On the one hand there is the self-preserving instinct of the ego to defend itself with great determination against any assault that threatens its integrity, on the other is the desire, or perhaps psychological necessity, to grow and develop. Without this a position of stasis would come about, the ego would stick to its own self-definition and there would be nothing to be served by going beyond this apparently cosy situation. As the shadow, or an aspect of the shadow, is recognised then the conflict between these two forces also emerges.

This can be an alarming experience and we may be quite disorientated for a while. For the counsellor a sound basic understanding of the task can act as an important reference point when little else seems fixed or sure. The confusion stems from the process by which our grasp of who we are is shifting. Inevitably this includes our professional selves and we may find ourselves wanting to gain a different or deeper understanding of what it means to be a counsellor. We may be drawn to start further training, seek out a more challenging supervisor for our therapeutic work or decide that the time has come to move our practice on in some other way. This might result in us taking on new work, starting to become involved in training and supervising others or undertaking research into aspects of the therapeutic process. Each of these is a possible response to our new-found commitment to face ourselves and move forward.

Incorporating the shadow

This is the next part of the radical psychological process that started with initial recognition of the shadow. When confrontation predominates then we are characteristically in a highly energised and turbulent state. As this subsides, as we become more reflective and accepting of what is taking place so we are moving into the phase that I am describing as 'incorporating'. This term is derived from the Latin word *corpus* meaning body and so suggests the shadow becoming part of the body or whole of who we are. It is unhelpfully simplistic to think that this means we are aiming for a state of singularity. Rather we are seeking to arrive at a state in which we can tolerate and embrace diversity within ourselves without this resulting in dramatic internal struggle. I can know myself to be genuinely caring and concerned on the one hand while also being capable of being ruthlessly disinterested in the plight of others on the other and for these two seemingly contradictory aspects of myself to coexist in relative harmony. This is the stage at which the shadow is no longer feared but rather respected and recognised as an important aspect of the functioning psyche.

It is important to be realistic from the outset and recognise that incorporating our shadow is a continuing process not a finite task. What we are aiming towards is an increasing overlap between our consciously identified sense of ourselves and our shadow. We become more willing and able to enter into what Johnson has described as the 'Mandorla' (1991: 97), which is the space created in the overlap between two circles. In this case it is the overlap of our identified self, or ego, and our shadow, as represented in Figure 4. The greater the degree of overlap the more we are able to access what has been in our shadow.

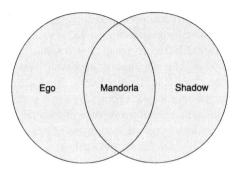

Figure 4 The Mandorla

Shadow as guide

Strictly speaking this is not a stage in itself but rather a possibility that opens up once we have incorporated a sufficient amount of our shadow into our sense of self. The information and wisdom that is contained in the shadow becomes increasingly accessible to us and can enhance our life and our work. Perhaps paradoxically the shadow does not lose its potential to be destructive but rather gains the possibility of being constructive. Our shadow has not changed as such, the shift has occurred in our attitude towards it. No longer is this an aspect of ourselves to be feared but rather we are receptive and perhaps even intrigued by it. We might imagine this as our standing at the edge of the Mandorla looking out towards our shadow. On occasions we see something that can help us in the task we undertake from our conscious selves.

The relationship between the stages

I trust it is clear that the stages are very different in nature and duration. The process of shadow formation takes place over many years and arguably can continue throughout our lifetime. It is interlinked with the stage of denial as this is what is required in order to keep shadow material unconscious. We may remain in a state of denial for decades and some will remain so throughout their whole lives.

When recognition starts to take place this signals, for most, the beginning of an inexorable process of further recognition, confrontation and incorporation. I think of this as parallel to the process of change in thermodynamic chemistry. Many chemical processes require initiating, for example by the application of energy from a heat source, traditionally the ubiquitous Bunsen burner. This is because there is insufficient energy in the system for the reaction to occur spontaneously: the chemicals are stable in their initial state under normal conditions. However, once a certain degree of chemical excitation has been reached as a result of energy being put into the system then the reaction is inevitable and unstoppable: the situation has become unstable (Laidler 1963). This I liken to the process of recognition: once we have a clear enough view of our shadow the reaction starts to occur within us and an irreversible process takes place that leads from recognition through confrontation to incorporation.

This movement is not absolutely inevitable at the outset of recognition. It is possible to pull back, to 'call on the moral intelligence to repair the rattle' as Bly (1988: 34) puts it. This is somewhat akin to the bargaining stage in the process of coming to terms with our own impending death. However, when sufficient recognition takes place that we come to accept the truth of what we are witnessing of ourselves the process gains considerable momentum. It is still possible to interrupt the process, perhaps through some major life crisis that serves to distract our attention sufficiently, but most move forward apace. The three connected stages of recognition, confrontation and incorporation can indeed be experienced as merging one into another in a relatively seamless process. In contrast to the earlier stages all three can be concluded over a period of months but it is more likely to take a few years as the initial momentum dissipates. Indeed it is arguable that we spend the rest of our lives in this process with the unrecognised elements of our shadow gradually shrinking in number and significance. Once sufficient of our shadow is incorporated it then becomes possible for our shadow to be a constructive or guiding influence and this is increasingly likely as more of our shadow is consciously embraced.

Stages of shadow framework and the counsellor's career

When we become counsellors we may be at any stage of the process of shadow formation and integration. There will be some who enter counselling when they have already come to know and incorporate much of their personal shadow. Others take up counselling when they are in the process of recognising, confronting and incorporating their shadow and will need careful support from trainers, supervisors and their own therapists to negotiate what is likely to be a difficult and confusing period. Similarly in need of support will be those who are catalysed into facing their shadow by the training process itself. Others will start out as counsellors while still in denial. They can expect to meet their shadow at some point as their work develops although this will not necessarily be early on in their practice. Indeed it is possible that the counsellor's shadow does not emerge until well on into their career. This contention is supported by examples of formal complaints of serious professional misconduct brought, and adjudged in the complainants' favour, against counsellors who have practised for a considerable number of years.

Aspects of shadow other than the personal shadow

I have already indicated that in addition to the personal shadow the counsellor has to contend with the shadow generated by taking on the counsellor persona. In addition to this there is also the collective shadow of counselling to be considered. We take up a restricted perspective if we view the personal shadow in isolation. However, this does create a dilemma, for until we have recognised, confronted and incorporated a significant amount of our personal shadow we do not have the means to consciously distinguish between these various forms of shadow. We may do so by an intuitive process but it remains difficult to distinguish between trustworthy intuition and untrustworthy projection. It would be neat and satisfying from a theoretical perspective to separate our personal shadow from the shadow created by the counselling persona, but from an experiential point of view it is not possible to make this distinction clear so I shall not attempt to do so in any systematic way in the next five chapters. Rather I shall leave these two aspects of shadow interwoven as this reflects what inevitably occurs when we take on the role of counsellor. I shall endeavour to keep separate the shadow of the client in the therapeutic field and the shadow of the profession and address these later as I believe this best reflects the order in which we are able to meet and recognise these different aspects of shadow. We do well to remember, however, that to some extent these distinctions between different parts of 'shadow' are somewhat artificial and simplistic attempts to give structure to areas of human experience that do not readily yield to any fixed description.

WHEN DEVELOPMENT DOES NOT TAKE PLACE

Earlier I made the assertion that development is a natural human process that will occur of its own volition. However, there are circumstances in which personal development is blocked, either permanently or temporarily. There are some who have such a degree of damage in their psyche that harsh survival decisions have had to be reached. For some such individuals impenetrable defences are erected as a means of salvaging some degree of order in a psyche that might otherwise descend into chaos. Some, but by no means all, who fit within a traditional model of psychopathology come within this group. Bollas suggests that 'mental illness is a freezing of the unconscious' (1995: 180) and that describes the situation well while being uncompromising in its starkness. For such individuals it is very much as if their psychological development has indeed been frozen. When this happens then the developmental process I am describing will not take place, as the necessary psychological stability is not present. Some among this group will be painfully aware of their shadow through the fears and fantasies that haunt them yet remain unable to incorporate their shadow into their sense of self.

We may all experience temporary periods in our lives when we do not have the resources to learn more about ourselves, when the demands of life are such that coping is the most we can aspire to. Such apparently barren times may turn out to be incubating future growth but equally they may simply be resting times on our journey.

3 Denying the shadow

This is the starting-point for each of us as adults. We have developed a personal shadow as we have grown through childhood and at this point we have little conscious grasp of what it contains. I have called this stage 'denying the shadow' because that is probably the most accurate psychological description. It would perhaps be more evocative to call it 'fear of the shadow' as this is the predominant emotional response for most. However, there are two other strong affective responses common at this stage: hostility and fascination. The hostility is generally expressed outwards onto others who are perceived to be the incarnation of the internal shadow that is unconsciously feared. The prudish person who has never had a satisfying sexual relationship who is scathing of the sexual indiscretions of others or the aggressive rebel who attacks anyone in power as being corrupt are stereotypical examples of this mechanism at work. In each case that which is denied within the individual is projected outward and then attacked in others.

Fascination with images of shadow is evident all around us. A brief glance at the popular titles in the fiction section of any bookshop or the films currently showing will invariably produce a number that are centred upon some struggle with evil. The examples may include monsters, ghouls and vampires, villains who must be identified and brought forward for judgement and punishment, political regimes that act with utter ruthlessness to maintain their power base and those who simply seem to delight in causing pain and misery. Such themes have been popular in literature and the arts for many centuries and can be thought of as a concern with the archetype of shadow.

For those not familiar with this term an archetype describes a fundamental pattern within the human psyche (Stevens 1990). Characteristically an archetype will be found recurring within many individuals across time and culture. It is a formative pattern within the human collective psyche, or collective unconscious[1] which then manifests itself within individuals.

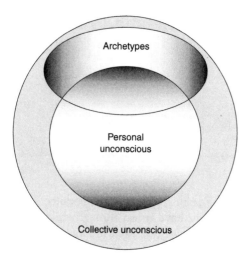

Figure 5 Archetypes and the unconscious

The relationship between archetypes, personal and collective unconscious is represented in Figure 5. Jung talks of archetypes as 'typical modes of apprehension' and goes on to state that 'whenever we meet with uniform and regularly recurring modes of apprehension we are dealing with an archetype' (1969: 137–8).

A considerable range of archetypes has been identified and explored, some of which are described primarily in a personified manner and others in terms of a pattern or force. Examples of those to be found in the first category include mother, child, trickster, Messiah and priest/priestess (Jung 1959a). Each of these are a manifestation of an identified archetype that can be readily ascribed to a type of person. However, it is a mistake to believe that the personification is the archetype. Thus the mother archetype is not simply represented by our biological mother but also by other powerful and nurturing female figures. They may be people we know such as teachers, significant family members or friends, or figurative as in the goddess or mother of Christ. In addition, institutions that inspire a sense of awe or devotion such as church, academy, or parliament may, for some, exemplify this archetype. For others, aspects of the natural world – the moon, sea, earth, fruiting plant – may be considered more apt examples.

Within the human psyche the image of absolute evil, of a destructive force of extreme potency, the archetype of shadow, does exist. There are examples of people acting in ways which would generally be accepted as evil: gruesome murders, dreadful physical and sexual attacks or mutilations of vulnerable victims, the horrors of the Holocaust or so-called 'ethnic cleansing'. The perpetrators of such acts apparently become the embodiment of this archetype either in a momentary act or a more general state. Being born in England in the 1950s there was no doubt for me and my childhood friends that Adolf Hitler was the embodiment of all that is evil. In other eras and in other cultures different figures will hold this position as the shadow archetype incarnate.

I feel sure that we all carry within us the potential for acts of great destruction even if we remain confident that there are no circumstances under which we would ever behave in this manner. Many of us get momentary glimpses of these possibilities within ourselves: the flash image of hurling the inconsolable baby I am carrying at the wall to silence her; the urge to force myself upon the lover who disdains my attentions; or the rage that wells up within me when an inconsiderate driver cuts across my path and the subsequent fantasy of ramming their car off the road. It is as if, in these moments of intense feeling, we can see across the divide within ourselves to view the violent and abusive possibilities that we contain. It is imperative to recognise that the personal shadow is not itself the embodiment of the shadow archetype. I find it helpful to consider the personal shadow and the shadow archetype as separate psychic entities that may share some characteristics but nevertheless remain distinct. The advantage I find in this schema, represented in Figure 6, is that the shadow archetype can then be placed within a community of archetypes, many of which have a somewhat more appealing nature! The personal shadow may then have identifiable components from a number of these archetypes but it is also the repository for unconscious material resulting from the particular experiences of that specific individual.

Fordham offers a somewhat different way of conceptualising the relationship between the personal shadow and archetypes, describing the shadow as 'the archetype nearest to the ego and is close to the repressed unconscious with which it regularly becomes integrated' (1986: 5). What is clear is that the personal shadow and the archetypal shadow material are not the same, although there will be some degree of merger and overlap in any one individual.

Clearly, counsellors are not immune to the effect of the shadow archetype but there are also a range of more apparently benign archetypes that pose a different sort of problem. One such is the trap of the Messiah or Saviour archetype which is particularly strong in Christian culture where the invitation is for each to find the Christ within. This is not, of itself, a necessarily dangerous quest and does lead many to acts of inspiring selflessness. The trap for counsellors is to forget that we are human, forget

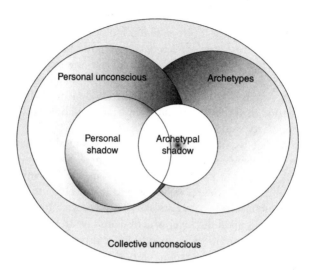

Figure 6 Archetypes and shadow

that we are a struggling damaged people and in this respect the same as our clients. This can be exacerbated when there is a transference component to the therapeutic relationship which places us in an archetypal position, as saviour or divinity as described by Gaultiere (1990). Unless well grounded in an understanding of the psychological processes that are occurring this can lead us into a dangerous self-delusion. Travelling down this path results in the inspiring desire to be an influence for good in the world becoming merely a device for egotistical grandiosity, fostering the self-deception of being somehow special.

This is a powerful trap posed by any archetype: to try to become the archetypal figure and thereby be possessed by a force that undermines our very humanity. An archetypal figure is a guide, a constellation of a particular aspect of human experience that reaches back into the depths of the history of our species upon this planet. But should we try to become that figure we become a caricature, losing much of our humanity in the process and becoming ridiculous in the eyes of others. The saviour archetype is not the only one to which counsellors are prone. Mother or father is another, particularly seductive to those who have spent many years in that biological role and may unwittingly be seeking to continue that function as a counsellor. That is not to deny how valuable the experience of being a parent can be as a counsellor (Guggenbühl-Craig 1971), but it is to be used within the context of full knowledge that this client is not my child but a responsible person who is to be assisted to find their own way forward in life.

There is a great deal of room for confusion in this area as at times the archetypal overlaps with human experience but at other times proves distant and unreachable. There is a delightful but sobering allegory of the process of archetypal possession in the highly original *Dune* trilogy (Herbert 1976). The character Alia is awakened to consciousness prematurely in her mother's womb and is immediately and directly aware of all her ancestors who continue to exist within her psyche. Eventually the pressure of this becomes unbearable and Alia chooses an alliance with one of the forebears within her. Initially this provides her with relief and a solution to her dilemma but gradually this unwholesome character takes increasing possession of her awareness and her downfall becomes inevitable.

This modern-day mythical story encapsulates key elements in the process of archetypal possession, for it emphasises how initially contacting the internal characters releases a great deal of energy that can be utilised to good effect. However, this gradually leads to downfall if the person becomes over-identified with a particular archetype and so loses touch with their personal identity. For the counsellor there are a number of archetypes upon which the role draws. In addition to saviour and parent there are also those of healer, shaman, priestess, priest, mage, witch, sage, guru[2] (Vigne 1991) and trickster (Jung 1959a) which may be equally important and seductive. Each of us is prone to being unduly influenced more by some of these than others as a consequence of our particular psychological predisposition and our cultural heritage. For me it is the priest archetype that I am especially susceptible to fall into. I particularly enjoy working with clients in the areas of their spiritual development and understanding which in itself is fine. However, I know that I can also take up a somewhat superior preaching tone, detaching myself rather than staying in therapeutic relationship, much as I caught myself doing in the incident I described in the opening of the Introduction. When this tendency comes to the fore it undermines the therapeutic relationship with clients and can be experienced as patronising or bombastic by supervisees, trainees and (I fear) readers!

It is important that safeguards are put in place that contain the dangers to both clients and counsellors from the intense unconscious psychological processes possible within a therapeutic encounter. These containers are particularly important when we are not yet able to recognise the contents of our personal shadow.

CONTAINING THE COUNSELLOR'S PERSONAL SHADOW

In this context a container is something that creates boundaries and has the capacity to hold the personal shadow of the counsellor within those boundaries. The concept of containment has a long history within the therapeutic world and is particularly well described by Winnicott (1965). He drew the parallel with the containing or holding function of the mother for her infant, providing the emotional security that enables the child to express his or her feelings in a context that is experienced as safe enough for these feelings not to overwhelm. The principle of containment for the personal shadow of the counsellor is somewhat different as there are two main purposes involved. The first is protection of the client from harm the counsellor may unwittingly do to them. The second is to protect the counsellor from the harm that being in this demanding role can create. Containers may also provide ways for the counsellor to start exploring shadow material in a way that is 'safe enough' for the psyche not to be overwhelmed by what is encountered.

Container one

The first container I want to consider is that of the practical structure within which the counselling relationship takes place. Thus counselling occurs within an agreed contract, has declared aims and purposes and takes place within clearly defined boundaries of time, place and confidentiality. These structures are intended to help in containing the client and act in conjunction with the containing impact of the counsellor themselves: '. . . both the frame and the therapist function as containers' (Gray 1994: 20). However, the structures also have the secondary function of acting as a container of the counsellor's shadow material. When these structures are not secure then there is considerably more opportunity for the personal shadow of the counsellor to take hold. When these structures are firmly in place then any action that steps outside of the structure is visible and can be examined for potential shadow involvement. For example, if a counsellor wants to see a client in a setting other than the consulting room the motivation for this proposal can be questioned. Is this evidence that the counsellor wishes to step outside the boundaries of the counselling role into some other form of intimate relationship? It may be a practically desirable step, perhaps because the client has become housebound or because a visit to a site of special significance to the client will assist the therapeutic process. Nevertheless, the possibility of shadow motivation needs to be considered so that it can either be set aside or dealt with.

To take another example: if the counsellor wants to go beyond the agreed purpose of the work with a particular client this again can be considered as possible evidence of a shadow agenda. Sometimes a client will touch us deeply and then it can be hard to let them go, to encourage them to move on when the work has been satisfactorily completed. At other times we may see further aspects of the client's life that we think they should address. But this is not counselling, it is taking over, presuming that we know what is best for this other person. A well-defined aim and purpose to the work of the counselling would show such incursions up for what they are. That is not to suggest that initial aims cannot be altered, on the contrary it is good practice to review and redefine the purpose of the work as it proceeds. However, to do so in dialogue with the client is a different matter from seeking to impose upon the client, and recognising this difference requires honest self-examination on the part of the counsellor, sometimes with suitable assistance.

Container two

The second container is provided by an awareness of the technique or craft of counselling. Every school or approach to counselling advocates a specific range of techniques or practices that are linked by theoretical constructs to a formulation as to how counselling is believed to actually work. For one practitioner it may be that therapeutic change is deemed to occur through the experience of an unconditionally accepting relationship with the counsellor (Mearns and Thorne 1988). How this counsellor acts towards the client then follows from this formulation. For another counsellor it may be that change is believed to be a consequence of working through hitherto unconscious material which is a consequence of some arrest in psychological development (Jacobs 1988). This may be done through specific techniques of free association, dream analysis or working from the assumption that what transpires within the therapeutic relationship is a manifestation of transference (Jacoby 1984). For a third practitioner it may be that change is deemed to occur as a consequence of reconstituting how the client constructs their image of themselves (Trower *et al.* 1988). Whatever the formulation and the techniques of a particular therapeutic approach knowledge and awareness of what these are provides a container. When the counsellor is aware of their technique and is intentionally practising this technique then their shadow is contained because the range of responses to the client are contained and the focus is clearly held upon the craft.

Kopp has used the delightful phrase 'assuming the posture' (1977) to describe the process whereby the therapist intentionally prepares themselves for the encounter with the client and maintains an awareness of their own task throughout the duration of the session. In order to achieve this the counsellor must start out with a clear understanding of the nature of their task. The counsellor who practices without this clarity leaves themselves vulnerable either to being drawn away from their task by the client or to their personal shadow taking over. This is undoubtedly a particular danger for those trainee counsellors unfortunate enough to undertake training that lacks a coherent theoretical framework. Some courses have at times been guilty of this, offering an incoherent set of different models. This slackness is sometimes justified in the name of eclecticism or disguised as integrative without the necessary foundation. Effective eclectic or integrative models are distinguished by having rigorously brought together the different strands to create a coherent theoretical and technical base.

I know of a number of counsellors working from home in private practice who develop rituals that they undertake before working with clients, somewhat more elaborate than merely reading through notes of the previous session. For example, some change their clothes, using a particular style or set of clothes as a reminder of their role much as a doctor or pharmacist might put on a white coat, a police officer a uniform or a judge a wig and gown. Others prepare the consulting room in particular ways, putting out clean paper, rearranging furniture or in my own case resetting an errant clock! These simple devices can help in taking up the posture: a reminder of what is about to be undertaken. In the early days of practice this deliberate effort to perform the counselling task can feel cumbersome and awkward and there is a temptation to consider it artificial, as if the client is being treated disrespectfully in some way. However, it is an important part of reminding ourselves that we are there to perform a demanding set of tasks in the service of this other person.

Container three

The third container is the formal one of counselling supervision. Regular attendance at supervision is a requirement of all UK counsellors who ascribe to the BAC Code of Ethics and Practice (BAC 1997). Effective supervision has at its heart the interests of the client with the needs and interests of the counsellor held in juxtaposition. As such, being alert to evidence of the shadow of the counsellor is one of the primary responsibilities of the supervisor and one of the primary tasks of supervision. It is by no means assured of success in this regard for the effectiveness of supervision is dependent to a large degree on the counsellor focusing attention on the client work where such difficulties may be present. Thus there is an inevitable degree of censorship, sometimes deliberate but more often unconscious. A well-developed trusting relationship between counsellor and supervisor will help to minimise this temptation to divert supervisory attention from areas that need to be examined. Rather supervision, at its best, becomes a place where the counsellor of integrity can bring their concerns and share them without undue fear of censure. This is often a great relief and can result in revitalisation for the practitioner as well as increased clarity about the therapeutic process. Supervision is also the place where the first two containers can be examined and if necessary sharpened up.

Hawkins and Shohet (1989) take Winicott's notion of containment and apply it to supervision using the parallel of the role of the father for the mother with an infant. The supervisor plays this supportive and containing function enabling the mother (counsellor) to put her energies into providing the emotional security for the child (client). A central part of this containment is provided through the supervisor themselves feeling secure in their role as:

> The sense of security of the supervisor can provide a means of containment for the insecurities of counsellors in relation to their counselling work. If the insecurities can be contained within supervision then this provides the supervisee with a safe place in which to experience and explore doubts and anxieties and thereby, it is hoped, provide a route through and beyond those insecurities.
>
> (Page and Wosket 1994: 112)

Additional containment is proved in supervision through the clarity of contract that can assist the counsellor to feel 'held'.

It must be accepted that merely attending supervision does not necessarily result in any significant benefit to either client or counsellor. It is the quality of work within the supervisory session that determines the effectiveness of the outcome. I am alarmed when I hear counsellors expressing dissatisfaction with their supervision but acknowledge a reluctance to challenge their supervisor. At worst supervision can be irrelevant, bombastic, undermining, collusive or indulgent. At best it is a powerful influence in the continuing development of the counsellor and facilitates thorough and critical self-reflection.

Container four

The fourth container is provided by the formal codes of practice that apply to the work of a counsellor. The majority of counsellors come within the purview of one or more professional codes of practice depending upon the country within which they work and professional body, or bodies, to which they belong. A code is simply a set of guidelines; nevertheless, it does provide a set of parameters and on occasions will have the effect of proscribing behaviour that otherwise might occur. A code also provides, as Bond (1993) has clearly set out, a framework within which the ethical aspects of a particular situation can be considered. As such it can provide a moderating influence: the over-anxious counsellor fearful for their depressed client may be discouraged from acting on their impulse to phone the client's doctor without further thought or discussion. The discussion such a counsellor needs to have before deciding upon any direct action would need to take account of their over-protective tendencies. The counsellor with a poor sense of boundaries and perhaps an over-inflated view of what they can achieve may be discouraged from agreeing to see the wife of their best friend as a client by reading the code of practice governing their work. They may not particularly agree with the admonishments to avoid overlapping personal and counselling relationships but may grudgingly be guided by them nevertheless. In these ways a code may act as a container, provided that it is read and understood. Codes also provide a container for the profession in that they provide the basis for dealing with those formal complaints that sometimes arise when the therapeutic relationship has broken down.

Container five

The fifth container is the personal therapy of the counsellor, if indeed they are in therapy. There is, as Guy states, 'a widely held belief among psychotherapists that personal therapy is desirable, if not necessary preparation for conducting psychotherapy' (1987: 58). Interestingly, this view is not particularly supported by research findings (Aveline 1990) but it is not surprising that as therapists we believe in the effectiveness of our own craft. There is debate about the necessity of every counsellor being in therapy and I find myself having three quite distinct responses to this question, each formed by viewing the debate from the perspective of different parts of my own experience. As a supervisor of counsellors I prefer my supervisees to be in therapy because it simplifies my task. I have on occasions exerted a degree of pressure on trainee counsellors to go into therapy if the course does not require this of them. This has not been an indiscriminate attitude on my part but rather a concern because of evidence that personal material is indeed leaking into their counselling work. Also as supervisor I have sometimes felt burdened by the amount of material I have been trying to hold on the supervisee's behalf. In contrast I have supervised one counsellor in whose work I had great confidence who had not received personal therapy. However, this person had come through a profound personal tragedy which had left a legacy of considerable depth of self-understanding. Thus there are occasional exceptions to my view as supervisor that it is generally very important for counsellors to have experience of being in therapy.

As a therapist I have had a small number of clients who have come to see me with some reluctance because it was a requirement of their counselling course. Although some useful work has resulted I have usually been left dissatisfied and troubled because the person has not, in my view, had a particularly rounded therapeutic experience. I am contrasting these experiences with those of working therapeutically with those trainee counsellors who are hungry to know more of themselves.

As a practitioner I have been in individual therapy for two periods totalling about four and a half years. At the time each was very significant for me as a person and as a practitioner. I entered therapy each time because I felt the need for myself and so was quite committed, although that didn't prevent me from trying out a considerable repertoire of prevaricating strategies once I had begun! The main focus was upon me as a person but occasionally I would take client work to explore how it was affecting me. I greatly valued the experience but I find it difficult to imagine that it could have been as valuable had I felt required in any way to be in therapy. Being responsible for setting up and maintaining the therapy week after week and being able to bring it to an end when I felt the time was right was an important aspect of the experience for me. I do not have one simple answer to this issue but I think that it is an important one which all within the profession and particularly those involved in the selection and training of new counsellors need to treat with seriousness.

From the point of view of containment, therapy can be double-edged in that it can stir up aspects of the personal shadow which hitherto have remained quiescent within the unconscious. However, having a regular opportunity to have our own needs given attention and affirmed in their own right often provides a safety valve so that pressure from the shadow does not build up to such an intensity as to force its way into the therapeutic work we are doing. Personal therapy provides us with a place outside our counselling work where we may legitimately talk about our experience of being a counsellor without jeopardising the confidentiality commitment to our clients. It is also an area in which our personal shadow can be recognised and accepted. There are parallels between supervision and the counsellor's personal therapy with the difference resting in intention: in supervision the intention is to improve the quality of work with clients, whereas in therapy the intention is to provide a safe facilitative environment in which the individual is him- or herself the primary focus of concern.

Container six

The sixth container is that of the personal life of the counsellor. The counselling work of each practitioner takes place within the wider context of that individual's life. If our personal life is rich and satisfying then it follows that many of our personal needs will be met. If we have a sound personal foundation then we are likely to be able to keep our work in perspective. Personal friendships have been described as 'one of the strongest staples for happy survival' (Coltart 1993: 99). Satisfying personal relationships should also preclude serious temptation to try to meet personal needs through our work which is one of the ways in which difficulties build. As such it provides a container for our personal shadow in as much as fewer needs will be seeking to find a way to be met. In contrast if our personal life is unsatisfactory, if needs for intimacy, social interaction and enjoyable activity are not being met we are far more vulnerable to our shadow clamouring for satisfaction.

Just as there are dangers for clients if our personal needs leak into counselling so too there are dangers for us if aspects of being in the role of counsellor leak into our personal lives. The psychological mindedness we develop as practitioners can be a danger to us as people. Many will be aware of those periods that many counsellors pass through when it seems impossible to turn off the psychological antennae. This can lead to an acute awareness of the nuances and unspoken communications of every conversation. For a while this can be fun and recognised as part of the learning involved in becoming a counsellor; however, it can also be alarming and disorientating as every passing comment seems loaded with multiple levels of meaning. This can also be quite disconcerting for those around us, perhaps leaving them feeling exposed or unduly scrutinised. It is an acute condition that many of us pass through for a period but it usually dissipates as we accommodate this new way of viewing the world around us.

Although this new perspective can be exciting and illuminating, perhaps providing much needed self-understanding, it may also carry a cost. This may come in the form of lost relationships if some people are no longer willing to be with us. This does occur, presumably because the changes in the person who is becoming a counsellor are uncomfortable for others in some way. I have known of people who I have lost touch with only to learn later that they became wary of me, feeling that I was always analysing them. At times this has caused me pain and resulted in the temptation to disclaim my profession in case it makes others circumspect with me.

There is another quite different potential cost: a loss of spontaneity. With increased awareness of the variety of ways in which what is said and done can be understood so can come a tendency to reflect unduly, detracting from immediate and unselfconscious response. This again may be an acute phase that is transitory but it can also become a more chronic state. For the counsellor who has become somewhat submerged in this way further personal therapy is perhaps not the best solution as it may exacerbate the situation. Rather some activity that fosters the desired characteristic of spontaneity is likely to have a beneficial effect. Such an activity, which can be anything from performing stand-up comedy to one of the martial arts, may assist in generating a capacity to 'switch off' from being a counsellor. These are but two examples of how the heightened awareness characteristic of a therapeutic practitioner can exact a price, alongside the personal development benefits it also offers.

As counsellors we deal variously with the boundaries between personal and professional life and these boundaries are likely to change over time. There may well be periods when life may be experienced as virtually seamless with little visible distinction between personal and professional aspects. Indeed for someone living in that way such terms as personal and professional life would probably seem quite superfluous. There may be other times when counselling is perceived very much as formal work to be kept quite separate from personal life. If this sixth container is to function there will need to be some attention paid to the overall context within which we fulfil our role.

Container seven

The seventh and final container is that of the organisation or network within which we operate. For many counsellors this is the informal compliment to the more formal support of supervision. Indeed many counsellors working within teams greatly value the *ad hoc* discussions that they are able to have with colleagues. It can be particularly good in containing the gossipy aspect that some of us may have in our shadows, for it provides a relatively safe forum to talk about some of what transpires with clients without constituting a breach of confidence. Without such an opportunity there may well be inappropriate leakage to friends or partners as the research by Baker and Patterson (1990) has shown. When counsellors work in a team they may have a confidentiality contract with clients that is team-wide so that such discussions, provided they do not trivialise or undermine clients, are included within the confidentiality net. Counsellors who do not work in teams may set up networks with other practitioners that serve some of the same functions of containment although negotiating confidentiality boundaries may be somewhat more problematic.

This container is more than simply an opportunity to talk about individual clients, indeed in many instances this will be considered outside of the confidentiality contract and avoided. Rather it provides the counsellor with a sense of being part of something beyond themselves. Working alone with clients in the consulting room can feel very isolating and can lead to an insidious distortion of perception. Just as doctors and health workers spend a lot of time with people who are ill or injured, police and lawyers with those who commit crime, so counsellors spend a lot of time with people who are distressed or disturbed. It would not be particularly atypical in one week for a full-time counsellor to see five people who were seriously abused or damaged as children, two who are deeply depressed, one who is in danger of starving to death as a consequence of eating difficulties, three who have been bereaved and another two whose partnerships or marriages are disintegrating. Doing this forty or more weeks out of a year can make it increasingly difficult to maintain a sense of perspective, to remember that this is not a representative cross-section of the total population. For the practitioner of a pessimistic or depressive nature the lack of such a perspective could result in the gradual development of a decidedly jaundiced view of the human condition.

In some settings the counsellor will have statistical evidence to indicate that their client group is but a small part of the total population. Thus student counsellors will know what proportion of the overall student group they see, workplace counsellors what part of the workforce and counsellors in health centres what fraction of the total patient group. This may help in retaining some perspective, a reminder that those in need of counselling are only a modest proportion of the total. However, such statistical evidence will not counterbalance the emotional impact we may experience if we find ourselves depleted or burdened by the suffering we witness in, and to some extent share with, those we counsel. The mutual recognition and support among colleagues involved in similar work can run much deeper than a simple statistical understanding and help us to maintain the necessary sense of perspective.

Being part of an organisation or network can assist in containing those elements of our personal shadow that may be stimulated by the potential loneliness of the role, as well as being intrinsically professionally pleasurable. If you are not part of a team or network you may be well advised to consider whether you do feel isolated in your work. If so you might want to invest the time and energy needed to access a support network or forum with other like-minded practitioners. When I was working in private practice I found it essential to be part of a local network of counsellors. We met for regular discussion about counselling issues, to share knowledge and experience and give each other support. There was also a peer supervision group in which client work could be explicitly discussed. The network acted as a means of making referrals so had the secondary advantage of being a source of clients and of other practitioners to whom clients could be referred. There are many such networks in existence and there are also some e-mail[3]-based discussion forums that serve a similar function to a limited extent. Where no suitable network exists it may well be feasible to set one up.

Summary

Taken together these seven containers: the practical structure; awareness of task; supervision; codes of practice; therapy; personal life; and team or network can serve an important function in minimising the detrimental effect of our personal shadow on our work with clients, particularly while we are in the stage of denial. They do more than this of course, protecting us from the dangers of the role and forming the foundation for good practice throughout our counselling career.

THE DEVELOPMENTAL IMPLICATIONS OF THIS STAGE

The practitioner who is still in a state of generalised denial of their shadow and who has not yet started to recognise in any detailed way the contents of their shadow is limited in their developmental potential. In relation to the schema offered by Skovolt and Rønnestad (1995) a counsellor still in this state will not be able to progress beyond the fourth stage as they are limited to working within a restricted technical frame. Any still in denial who do try to work beyond the strictures of their initial training are very vulnerable to their shadow intervening. The work of those involved in investigating and processing formal complaints within the therapeutic professions often involves counsellors in this category. Such practitioners have started to move into more experimental ways of working without recognising the difference between true flexible response to the client and gratification of personal needs or desires.

Many of us have moved beyond a generalised state of denial but are still afraid of our shadow. This may indicate that there are other components of our shadow that we have yet to identify and are impinging upon our work with clients. It may also simply be a reflection of the reality that there will always be aspects of ourselves that remain unconscious. As such, a degree of cautious respect for what remains hidden to us seems a wise attitude to maintain.

4   Recognising the shadow

When personal shadow material emerges in any act the person engaged in that act will inevitably be unconscious of the underlying motivations involved and may prefer to remain in apparently blissful ignorance. However, any thought, feeling or behaviour that is driven by unconscious forces also provides an opportunity for growth, a window through which the shadow is visible, if sometimes only for a moment. As counsellors we will probably all have felt the frustration of working with a client who insists on remaining oblivious to the impact of their unconscious in their everyday life, one example of this being those individuals who seem able to form relationships only with partners who treat them appallingly. For some this may happen over and over again before they are willing to consider the possibility that they may be playing some part in this process. It often remains a long road from that first recognition until the stage when the pattern can be broken, either by opting to be single or by forming a relationship in which they are treated respectfully. In the meantime as the counsellor we may have to endure repeated occasions of helplessly watching as our client once more creates a situation that results in great suffering and in some cases physical danger for them. With a person in such a predicament we have to remind ourselves that they will only be able to recognise the pattern when they are ready. Meanwhile if we try to describe what we see them doing before they are ready our good-intentioned observations are likely to be transformed into self-recrimination. This in turn can further fuel the underlying belief that they are a bad person and deserve to be treated as such. Great patience is required, for it is seldom predictable when a particular individual will start to recognise the unconscious at work in their lives.

IDENTIFYING CLUES

This is equally true for counsellors as it is for clients: we may be oblivious to the repeating patterns that would lead us to our personal shadow if we but noticed. Sometimes the shadow seems to leave clues, almost as if we try to trap our conscious selves into having to accept the influence of our unconscious upon our actions. Let me illustrate this with the example of a painful episode in my life some years ago. At the time I was living with my girlfriend, who I shall call Elaine. My work commitments were such that I felt tied to the town I lived in for the foreseeable future. Meanwhile Elaine was offered an exciting opportunity to further her career but it involved moving abroad. She prevaricated, wanting not only to be with me but also to take up the invitation that had been made. After some time I could no longer tolerate Elaine's indecision or my pain and anger that she was considering leaving me. I did not find a satisfactory way to express these feelings but rather brought our relationship to an end, pre-empting what I anticipated Elaine would do. She left and in the course of making the practical decisions involved in the parting I agreed to look after her young cat called N'Assarudin.[1] This arrangement was to avoid N'Assarudin being put through unpleasant quarantine procedures and also because Elaine was unsure that she would be moving into accommodation where he would be welcome. I felt quite willing to have N'Assarudin: I liked him and already had a cat of my own.

A few weeks after Elaine had departed I went on a work-related trip, arriving back home late one night. The next morning I turned on the automatic washing machine and to my horror realised that N'Assarudin had managed to get in with the clothes. Because of the door safety lock it took a few minutes to get N'Assarudin out and, despite his protestations, rinse him down. Three days later N'Assarudin died, having being poisoned by the detergent he had absorbed through his skin.

I would have liked to have believed that this was just a very unfortunate accident and not some shadowy acting out of my resentment and hostility towards Elaine. However, there were two glaringly clear sets of clues pointing inexorably to my unconscious connivance in this 'accident'. The first was that during my trip away I had stayed with some colleagues who had a number of cats and in the course of a conversation we had discussed in some detail the dangers of washing machines for cats. I also knew that I had acted in an unusual way: I habitually put washing into the machine at the point I was going to switch it on yet on this occasion had put the clothes in the machine the night before and left the door open. For me the most difficult aspect of this whole episode was that at the point I realised the results of my shadow in action the damage was already irreversibly done: the poison was already in N'Assarudin's body.

Thankfully shadow-driven actions do not always have such grim consequences and are not always so irrecoverable. The action cannot be undone once performed but sometimes the consequences can be ameliorated. It was hard for me to deal with the guilt I felt about my central role in N'Assarudin's death. However, this precipitated me into entering individual therapy so I did salvage something constructive from this horrible event.

A second example of the shadow leaving clues as to its part in events is to be found in the experience of Julia and her therapist. Julia struggled with a self-esteem that had been bruised, and eventually badly damaged, by the repeated experience of being undermined and discounted by her parents. She described herself as 'the runt of the litter', being the youngest of four children and finding few areas in which she could achieve as well as her siblings. She made many attempts during her upbringing to incur the pleasure of her parents, particularly her mother, but had eventually given up in the face of repeated failure. She came into therapy in her early thirties, having decided that it was time to make some changes to a life that she found grey and unsatisfactory. Some time after starting therapy Julia had discovered a delight in painting and drawing so was avidly attending local adult classes in both. With some trepidation Julia suggested to her therapist, Anne, that she might bring some of her artwork to explore during their sessions. This was agreed and it was also decided that the sessions would be extended to one and a half hours to give more time for this different way of working. In the second of these longer sessions Anne became muddled over time and brought the work to an end fifteen minutes early. After Julia had left Anne realised what had occurred and felt horrified at her inadvertent 'mistake'.

In this example the first clue lies in the information Anne already had about Julia, particularly her repeated experiences of being discounted by her parents. The other clue is that when Anne realised what had happened, the strength of her feelings was out of proportion to this having been a simple mistake. Nevertheless the early ending of the session cannot be satisfactorily explained when only considering the event from the perspective of Anne's shadow. A broader model is required that does not treat the shadow of the counsellor in isolation, as if the client is simply a passive participant. Such a counsellor-centred model is patently unsatisfactory: counselling only has any meaning and purpose if it is intended to be a therapeutic arena for the client. In order for it to be so the client must be free to bring her shadow material into the consulting room (we shall explore the theme of the client's shadow in more depth in Chapter 8). Indeed for many clients working upon unconscious material, be it from their shadow or other aspects of their personal unconscious, is a fundamental aspect of the task and for some it will form the central purpose for being in counselling. Consequently the potential complexity of an actual counselling situation must take into account the possibility of interactions between the shadow of the counsellor and that of the client. Only then does it become possible to propose any sensible meaning to the event that transpired for Julia and Anne.

Transference and countertransference

In the psychoanalytic tradition the interaction between the unconscious of the therapist and the client has been examined using the concepts of transference and countertransference (Jacoby 1984). Not all transference or countertransference originates in the shadow; the shadow is not the only content within the unconscious; however, these concepts are applicable to shadow material. In general the term transference is used to describe material from the unconscious of the client that is being transferred onto the counsellor. Often this is historic relationship material, so the client might unwittingly behave towards the counsellor 'as if' the counsellor were some significant figure from the client's past. In so doing the client re-enacts his or her part in this past relationship and thereby makes this material available to be worked on as part of the counselling process. The same phenomenon can take place with material from a present, rather than past, relationship. In either event it remains a matter of conjecture and theoretical preference as to whether this process is believed to occur at the behest of some purposeful guide within the psyche of the client or simply as a compulsive response in settings such as that provided by counselling.

In many instances the counsellor will experience an emotional response to transference material from the client. Comprehending these responses and using the understanding of them in a therapeutically purposeful manner is complex. To do so as counsellors we must first reach a view as to the source of our emotional experience. But how are we to know with any degree of certainty if our feelings towards the client are a response to the transference material the client is directing towards us? It is equally possible that our feelings are a manifestation of material from our own unconscious intruding upon the counselling relationship. To aid in clarifying this very important distinction two types of countertransference have been defined: 'syntonic countertransference' and 'illusory countertransference' (Fordham 1960). Syntonic countertransference describes a direct response to the transference material being directed towards us by the client. Illusory countertransference is our own unconscious material, probably from our shadow, that we are directing towards the client. Thus illusory counter-transference is 'counter' in that it flows in the opposite direction to that

Figure 7 The countertransference continuum

in which transference moves. This is quite different to syntonic counter-transference which is directly responding counter to the transference of the client. Illusory countertransference is not necessarily responsive as its source lies within the unconscious of the counsellor. Any counter-transference action can be thought of as belonging somewhere on the continuum indicated in Figure 7.

We can now return to the example of Anne and Julia, as we have the concepts needed to consider what took place. The most appealing hypothesis is that when Anne ended the session fifteen minutes early she was acting in a manner that reflected how Julia's mother had behaved. When Julia had wanted to get extra attention for her artwork Anne had ended up depriving her of that additional time, even though this time had been negotiated and agreed. This hypothesis suggests that there was some transference from Julia to which Anne had unconsciously reacted. This aspect of Anne's response is syntonic countertransference and is 'concordant'[2] because what Anne does complies with Julia's unconscious expectation. However, it is not sufficient to say that Anne simply reacted to Julia's transference because this doesn't explain why Anne did react in this way. It was not simply syntonic countertransference but had an illusory countertransference component also. What transpired when this situation was explored in supervision was that Anne harboured some resentment towards Julia's request for a longer session and it was this that Anne was inadvertently expressing when she apparently muddled the time. In this example, what occurred between Anne and Julia rests somewhere in the middle area of the countertransference continuum. The intensity of Anne's feeling of horror when she realised what had happened can be interpreted as her response to recognising her shadow at work. This sense of horror seems to be quite a common occurrence in the moment of shadow recognition.

In my own practice both as a counsellor and as a supervisor of other counsellors I have yet to identify any examples of pure syntonic counter-transference. This may be a limitation in my understanding of the term (or of myself) but I cannot conceive of countertransference that is entirely rooted within the client's unconscious. It seems to me to be the case that any transference that elicits an emotional, cognitive, fantasy or behavioural response from the counsellor must have found something within that counsellor's psyche with which to resonate, often within their personal shadow.

In contrast it is feasible for pure illusory countertransference to occur when counsellors engage in activities that come into play regardless of the agenda the client brings. An example within this is provided by David, a counsellor who demanded that all his clients displayed evidence that the counselling was having a positive effect. For many clients this had little discernible impact: they did find the counselling helpful and so David's need was met, with most clients probably not realising that they had performed this gratuitous service for him. However, those of his clients with more intractable difficulties were subjected to an increasing pressure to achieve some identifiable progress. This pressure was initially reported as a sense of frustration or disapproval emanating from David towards the client. For some this moved on to David questioning the usefulness of con-tinuing counselling, which clients experienced as a threat that counselling would be withdrawn if they could not produce evidence of progress. Inevitably a degree of 'flight into health' (Casement 1985: 40) took place.

This particular manifestation of generalised illusory countertransfer-ence was particularly difficult to untangle for two reasons. First, for each individual client their sense of being put under pressure could easily be attributed to a projection of their own internal self-criticism. It was only when it came to light that a number of clients were sharing a similar experience of David that the illusory countertransference started to become visible. This happened because David worked in an agency where clients regularly had contact with a range of other professionals, some of whom picked up the dissatisfaction among his clients. Second, the diffi-culty in bringing this problem to light was that David worked in a setting where there was considerable pressure on resources and every effort was made to keep counselling relatively brief. Thus the legitimate needs of the service dovetailed with the unconscious need of this particular counsellor. The hallmark of this set of illusory countertransference activities is that they pervade all the client work of the practitioner. This particular aspect of David's personal shadow was present with every client.

There is another type of illusory countertransference activity in which the client unwittingly acts as a trigger to the unconscious material of the counsellor. Helen is a counsellor who had the capacity to be experienced by clients as quite critical. It took Helen quite a while to come to recognise this and only after it arose now and then that her supervisor felt that Helen was talking in quite a criticising way about a particular client. When

Helen and her supervisor examined this with some care what emerged was a pattern of this happening with female clients who presented themselves in quite a passive way. Helen was able to identify that she did feel critical towards these clients and went on to address this in personal therapy. In so doing she was able to become more accepting of her own tendency to be passive and in turn to be more compassionate towards the passivity she met in some clients. The primary characteristic of this form of illusory counter-transference is that it does not emerge with all clients but is restricted to those who have the necessary characteristics to act as a catalyst. This type of illusory countertransference falls somewhere towards the illusory end of the continuum as it is neither entirely syntonic nor entirely illusory but does emanate from the counsellor. I trust that this will not be mis-interpreted as my blaming clients for being subject to some inappropriate activity by counsellors as that is not my intention. There are undoubtedly occurrences of malpractice where the counsellor can rightly be held entirely responsible and culpable for what transpired. However, when the unconscious demands of such a practitioner come to light, in supervision or in a complaint, it will be because the shadow of the counsellor has succeeded in eliciting some response from the client. Take for example a counsellor willing to prey upon the emotional vulnerability of clients in order to gain some personal satisfaction. A client who is susceptible may well succumb to the advances made, believing that some genuine offer is being made to them; however, the client who is not susceptible in this way can be expected to brush aside the overtures, and indeed the counsellor may well sense that such an individual is unsuitable quarry and curb their desires. This dynamic results in the cruel irony that it is the most vulner-able clients who are most likely to be abused by an unscrupulous or dangerous practitioner.

Returning to the notion of a continuum, once identified, countertrans-ference phenomena can be placed somewhere along this line. This is not an intrinsically useful process but it does serve as a representation and can lead into the process of sifting through the material, distinguishing between that which belongs with the counsellor and that which belongs with the client. As counsellors we can then start to address our part of what occurred and also think through appropriate therapeutic strategies for working with the client's material. I trust that I have made it clear, by examining transference and countertransference processes in some detail, that recog-nising the presence of our personal shadow in our work with clients is often difficult and requires careful analysis and reflection. It is not usually glaringly obvious, tending rather to be hazy but with a degree of familiarity or a ring of truth when we name what we think may have occurred.

Identifying the primary source

To illustrate the difficulties involved in this process and to identify some criteria that help to determine the source of countertransference let us consider the example of Sue who is counselling Robert. One day Robert arrives for the counselling session late, makes no apology and starts eating sandwiches with an offhand remark that he has not had time to stop all morning. He goes on to be very disparaging about his colleagues at work and his previous therapist who, Robert says, just sat there looking bored. Sue asks if that is directed towards her. Robert says not but then asks where Sue thinks the counselling is heading. At this point she gets quite angry and states that she would like Robert to think about what he wants from counselling as he doesn't appear to be taking it very seriously at the moment. Robert gets very angry saying he doesn't come to be abused and for Sue to dump her anger on him. Sue remains angry while feeling rather shocked that she is so heated, as if she is both angry and simultaneously witnessing the scene from a detached perspective. They finish in an uncomfortable silence, confirm their next appointment and Robert leaves. Reflecting upon the session later Sue perceives that Robert did behave in a provocative manner but nevertheless feels that her level of anger was decidedly disproportionate to the situation. She might also have taken her sense of detachment at the time as a clue as to the presence of her shadow. This experience of being particularly detached from ourselves seems to be quite common during a period when we are being influenced by our shadow.

Having recognised that her own material came into the session in some way, it becomes very important for Sue to consider this interchange in more depth. She can do this by herself but it is preferable to seek out the assistance of a third party, provided that this can be achieved without going outside the boundaries of confidentiality that she has contracted with Robert to maintain (Bond 1993). Sue's supervisor is the obvious and most legitimate third party but this occurrence might also be reflected upon in informal supervision with a colleague or in her own therapy. Her own therapist is a quite appropriate source of support as Sue has already recognised that her personal shadow played some part in the interaction. Sue would need to be aware that her therapist would be primarily concerned with her needs stemming from the encounter, leaving Sue to take responsibility to see that Robert's needs were adequately addressed.

The purpose of exploring this situation, by whatever means Sue chooses, is to find a way forward in the therapeutic work that is in Robert's best interests. In this particular situation this would involve investigating what had occurred with a view to coming to some working understanding of the underlying dynamic process. Such an understanding then provides a foundation upon which Sue can base plans as to how she will proceed with Robert.

The first question that might be considered is whether or not what had happened with Robert is a familiar situation in Sue's counselling work. If indeed Sue often finds herself feeling angry in this manner with her clients then this would point very strongly to an illusory countertransference of the generalised type. This occurrence with Robert would then be seen as further evidence that Sue's shadow was encroaching into her work regardless of the client she was working with. Taken alongside other similar incidents this is then a serious matter in terms of Sue's continued practice and effective measures would need to be taken in order to minimise the danger of harm to her clients. It is very probable that if this is the case, given the nature of such shadow material, Sue will not readily see her own unconscious process at work. In such a situation it would probably fall to her supervisor to both recognise the emerging pattern across a number of Sue's counselling relationships and confront Sue with this information. One of the reasons why it is so important for there to be a well-formed 'basic affective relationship' (Page and Wosket 1994) between counsellor and supervisor is that it provides a foundation upon which such a confrontation can take place with a reasonable likelihood of success.

If both Sue and her supervisor are able to agree that this was not a typical occurrence then attention can turn to the nature of Sue's felt experience, both during the session with Robert and subsequently. In considering her emotional responses to Robert within the session itself it is useful to explore to what extent the feeling quality was familiar to her. Thus the question might be posed: 'Is the way you felt angry with Robert the way you usually feel when you are experiencing what you call "anger"?' To be able to give a material answer to this question Sue needs to be quite sophisticated in her understanding of her own affective experience. She would need to be sufficiently familiar with the range of her emotional experience to adjudge whether the feelings she was experiencing with Robert came from within her own feeling 'palette'. If it did not, if she experienced a sense of unfamiliarity in the feeling, then this would be persuasive evidence that what took place was strongly influenced by Robert's unconscious material. There have been occasions in my own practice when I have experienced feelings in working with a client that I do not recognise as falling within my usual range of affective responses. It is as if what I am feeling is somehow of a different shade to the one I would expect: different in some quality to that in which this feeling is familiar to me. In psychodynamic parlance such an experience might be deemed to fall within the definition of syntonic countertransference or it might be considered to be an example of a phenomenon known as projective identification.[3] The precise conceptual definition may be helpful in identifying the unconscious mechanisms present: however, such definition is secondary in the quest to clarify the primary source of the unconscious material present in the exchange between counsellor and client.

The third aspect of the interaction that can be usefully examined concerns what I term the 'dissipation rate' of the felt experience. This dissipation rate, which those of a scientific disposition might want to think of as the 'half-life'[4] of the feeling, is the rate at which the intensity of the emotional experience decreases over time. Again this is a relatively crude and subjective measure but nevertheless provides further information about the nature of Sue's affective experience. The underlying assumption is that feelings that emerge as a direct response to the transference material of the client and have little or no corresponding resonance within the counsellor will usually lose intensity quite quickly after the session is concluded. In contrast, feelings that may be triggered by the client's work but have a strong emotional basis within the psyche of the counsellor can be anticipated to diminish much more slowly. That is not to suggest that the counsellor will simply continue to have a constant level of feeling, but rather that the feelings will be available to be restimulated. In Sue's case it would be important to notice whether she again feels strength of anger if she sits and reflects upon the session, recollects the situation in supervision or sees Robert again for a subsequent session. If this does happen then this suggests that there is a significant degree of Sue's personal psychological material, her shadow, present in her feelings of anger towards Robert. The longer the period since the session that restimulation can occur the deeper within Sue's psyche the roots of her anger can be deemed to reach.

Each of these three measures – the generality of the emotional experience across a group of clients; the degree of familiarity of the feeling quality; and the rate of dissipation – provides information about the primary source of the emotional material within the counselling situation. Additional perspectives can also emerge through examination of a range of elements of the relationship between client and counsellor. Hawkins and Shohet (1989), writing about supervision, have described in detail six levels at which the therapeutic process can be examined, of which the counsellor's countertransference is just one.[5] Investigation of this sort requires considerable self-awareness and honesty on the part of the counsellor. The counselling material that is being scrutinised is usually accessed through the counsellor and so may be filtered or censored, consciously or unconsciously. It often requires acuity and sensitivity on the part of the counsellor's supervisor, assisting the counsellor to recognise and take responsibility for his or her personal shadow involvement with the client when this is the case. For any counsellor who is committed to their work and has a strong sense of personal integrity it can be very hard to countenance the possibility that shadow material is affecting, and possibly causing harm to, the client.

INHIBITION AGAINST RECOGNITION

In each of the examples in this chapter there is some inhibiting factor that tends to discourage recognition. In the first example of the death of N'Assarudin it is the shame of having caused the death of an animal in my care. In each of the other examples the counsellor has felt, expressed or manifest something that does not fit within our everyday understanding of the role of counsellor. It is not usually considered part of the counselling role to resent a client as Anne did, make personal demands of clients as David did, criticise passive clients as Helen did or be very angry with a client as Sue was. If these counsellors are to recognise their shadow involvement in what occurred they have to accept that they have not performed the role as they would wish. This combines with any personal inhibition, any guilt or shame, the individual might have to face about what they have felt or done.

I anticipate that we could each identify a list of feelings, thoughts or behaviours in an order of increasing unacceptability. This is not restricted to counsellors as everyone develops moral codes about what is and is not acceptable. When I run training events in counselling I sometimes invite participants to identify, from an extensive list, feelings that they consider unacceptable to have towards another person.[6] With some groups I have asked that they consider feelings they find unacceptable towards any other person and with other groups I have asked that they think specifically about feelings they find it unacceptable to have towards clients. While I have not systematically recorded the results (although it would be interesting to know what would emerge if this was done as a formal piece of research) I have been struck by some common themes in the responses. Those groups reporting feelings they consider unacceptable towards others in general have typically included envy, hate, jealousy, loathing and disinterest among their most common responses. The same feelings are also common for those reporting the feelings that they consider unacceptable towards clients but there is frequently the addition of sexual desire or arousal. This is not particularly surprising as the proscription of sexual activity between counsellors and their clients is general if not universal. Probably because of this, feelings of sexual desire towards clients have something of the quality of 'taboo' as Freud (1985: 71) describes it: a mixture of the sacred and forbidden. It follows that if we do not allow ourselves the feelings of sexual desire towards clients we do not have to deal with the discomfort they create.

I had a supervisee, Simon, come to see me who was clearly very anxious about a particular piece of work with a client. It was really hard for him to describe what occurred, being overwhelmed for a while by his fear of what he was about to divulge. To put this in context, I had been supervising Simon for a number of years, he was an experienced counsellor, I had a high regard for the quality of his work and trusted his integrity as a practitioner. Nevertheless, it was remarkably difficult for him to describe what had taken place. It transpired that he had suddenly experienced powerful erotic feelings in the middle of the sixth or seventh session with this client. We established that Simon had never had such feelings towards this client previously and the feelings dissipated by the end of the session. After careful examination we were both reasonably sure that these feelings were predominantly syntonic countertransference connected to the client starting to uncover her sexual frustration in her marriage. The work with the client proceeded well with Simon basing his approach on that hypothesis.

Simon did explore the source of his anxiety about his own feelings towards his client. He was able to identify some degree of sexual repression from his somewhat morally restrictive upbringing. However, neither he nor I were satisfied that this was a complete explanation: his fear had an intensity that seemed out of proportion to what he could connect with in his personal shadow. I suspect that in this particular instance his fear was a result of a resonance between his personal shadow and the client's material. In addition there is a further resonance with the widespread concerns which exist within the counselling field and beyond about potential sexual exploitation of clients. These concerns are well founded as there are instances of serious sexual abuse and exploitation of clients by counsellors (Rutter 1989; Russell 1993). This can lead, however, to important information about the therapeutic work being discarded because of a generalised fear and resulting injunction.

Another potential consequence to this injunction is that it can discourage the very important explorations of sexual feelings towards clients that counsellors need to undertake. If we do not explore this area then aspects of our sexuality that reside in our shadow may be left until some difficulty occurs with a client. I do not believe that sexual feelings in themselves represent a threat of harm to clients. Indeed sexual attraction from either party is a normal aspect of many human relationships and any attempt to exclude this possibility from counselling relationships seems a sad attempt to sanitise what should be a rich and significant relationship.

I am not advocating that we tell our clients if we find them attractive as I doubt this would have any therapeutic value in most cases and will inevitably create many difficulties. Rather I am proposing that as counsellors we are honest with ourselves, and our supervisors, about the nature and quality of feelings we have for our clients. In my view the danger for clients exists when such feelings are not recognised for what they are, when clients are used as objects to gratify our sexual feelings or when we are ourselves out of relationship with some aspect of our sexuality.

I am reminded of a trainee counsellor, Pat, who presented himself for therapy. Initially he simply told his counsellor that he wanted to have the experience of being a client. However, he soon started talking about himself, at first in quite a superficial way describing course work concerns and then moving on to his frustrations in personal relationships where he felt he could never get close. In doing so he was moving through the 'levels of disclosure' described by Cox (1978) until he reached the level three disclosure that he was deeply concerned about his sexuality. He described frequent masturbation using erotic homosexual imagery, both photographic and fantasy, with strong dominance and submission themes and an undertone of violence. Once Pat talked about his sexual activity and the associated guilt it became possible to start to access some of the memories and experiences that linked with the themes in his erotic fantasies.

What became apparent as the discussions progressed was how much Pat considered this homosexually oriented aspect of himself as 'other' with no place in his self concept. He found it morally unacceptable and wanted it to go away, to not exist any more. For some time he was very resistant to the possibility of it being an important part of who he is. At this point it can be said that Pat was starting to recognise and bring out in the open this aspect of his shadow. He did go on to accept it as part of himself and as he did so this 'other' part of himself diminished and the compulsion to masturbate subsided. This is an example of a counsellor who courageously faced up to an aspect of his sexuality that caused him serious difficulty. I have little doubt that had Pat not done this work in therapy he would have been in considerable trouble when faced with a male client he found attractive. This would have triggered a powerful sense of self-disgust and Pat would have struggled to stay in a therapeutically constructive relationship with the client. He remains prone to these difficulties arising because it is unlikely that he has completely dealt with the internal conflict from which all this stemmed; however, his new understanding equips him for occasions when the conflict emerges again.

I have explored sexuality as an example of the potentially inhibiting effect upon shadow recognition of the role itself because this is a difficult area for many counsellors. As a result it is prone to being placed in the role shadow as we endeavour to turn ourselves into asexual beings when we are with clients. We can be tempted to do this in order to avoid having to deal with the tensions it creates when we recognise feelings towards clients that we are not going to act on. Any area of human relationship that does not readily fit within the counselling role can be similarly treated and create an inhibition to recognising our personal shadow.

DEVELOPMENTAL IMPLICATIONS OF THIS STAGE

From a developmental perspective recognition of our own shadow at work is essential if we are to move into the more flexible and creative ways of working with clients. However, this is the first of a number of stages we need to move through and therefore care is required. To start with there is likely to be a lack of balance in our understanding, with some practitioners tending to fear that almost everything that occurs has its roots in their shadow. For such counsellors this is likely to be an anxiety-laden and difficult time and sensitive supervision encouraging a broader view will be helpful. In contrast others will tend to assume that most of what occurs starts from their clients. This can lead to some of the counsellor's own psychological material wrongly being attributed to clients. Typically counsellors reacting in this way will be prone to perceiving their clients as manipulative, devious, threatening, resistant, stuck or uncommitted to the work. While all of these are possible with occasional clients unless practising in a particularly difficult environment where clients are coerced into counselling this will generally be rare. Such practitioners need to be assisted to fully face what they are finding in themselves and may have to be actively encouraged, required even, to enter therapy for themselves.

One of the defensive positions which can be quite appealing in this stage is that of naivety: assuming that 'the client is always right', with little or no critical appraisal of what is being presented. This has quite an alluring and seductive quality because it allows us to take up an idealistic position and in so doing avoid the discomfort with which a more realistic practitioner has to struggle at times. Although it is attractive this position is very restrictive as it denies that the client has their own shadow. There are various reasons why this denial takes place: it allows us also to deny our own shadow; it avoids the necessity of grappling with occasional scepticism towards clients and therefore relinquishes the responsibility for confrontation; and it can lead to a cosy, comfortable, counselling relationship.

The naive position I am describing is an unfortunate caricature of the deeply authentic person-centred practitioner. The naive counsellor is generally not truly in relationship with the client (Shainberg 1983) for they are not willing to see fully the client for the person they are, preferring a sanitised version of their own devising. As such, this is quite a narcissistic state, undermining of useful therapeutic work. The true person-centred practitioner is in relationship with both the light and dark sides of the client and is willing to engage with either as appropriate (Mearns and Thorne 1988).

5 Confronting the shadow

In a number of the examples considered so far the shadow has emerged without any warning, as if it has of its own volition determined that it is time to move into the visible light of consciousness. It is not, of course, that our shadow decides that it is time to become conscious, but rather that we are willing and able to perceive something that until now we have kept hidden from ourselves. However, from the perspective of consciousness it is a passive process, we experience it as happening to us because at this point the shadow is 'other': it is not experienced as part of ourselves. This sense of 'other-ness' is usually profound as it is the basis upon which the split between shadow and ego has been built.

For some this meeting with the shadow is a single moment of blinding illumination, a Road to Damascus[1] experience. A classical example is the seemingly devoted parent and faithful husband or wife who suddenly falls in love with someone else and starts a passionate affair that eventually leads to the break-up of the family. If this individual has always believed themselves incapable of such behaviour then it will be a dramatic awakening of what has hitherto lain dormant. Such a person is being confronted forcibly with a passionate side to their nature that may well have dissipated in the original marriage relationship as can happen under the weight of the demands of parenthood or simply with years of familiarity. They are also faced with their capacity to betray and abandon those to whom they would previously have said, in all sincerity, they were utterly committed.

For others, beginning to consciously recognise and accept the shadow is a more gradual process. It seems that some people grow up with a recognition that an 'other' aspect of personality exists so that the notion of a personal shadow is relatively easy to accept. Such a person may already have grasped the notion of shadow so that when relatively minor examples emerge it is possible for these aspects of self to be considered and integrated. This does not preclude this individual from intense psychological struggles before being willing to face some of the more deeply embedded elements of personal shadow. Indeed I have come across a few people who are apparently very aware of their own shadow side only to later discover that in some areas of their life, typically in intimate relationships, their behaviour is very hurtful and destructive. For such individuals it is as if the apparent self-awareness they display is a ploy, a means of distracting attention away from other areas of their life where the shadow is rampant. Such a degree of splitting is indicative of quite a deep-seated psychological disturbance (Asper-Bruggisser 1987). Thus it is important not readily to equate some degree of self-awareness with the psychological maturity that results from ownership and integration of major components of personal shadow.

Starting to recognise our own shadow may happen, then, as a result of a dramatic and life changing moment or it may be a gradual unfolding process. Once the first conscious encounter with our personal shadow has taken place then a possibility opens up not to simply wait passively for the next time but to decide to turn around and seek out what else remains hidden. This turning point, when it is recognised that running away from the shadow is no longer an effective strategy, is delightfully described in Ursula Le Guin's modern fantasy *A Wizard of Earthsea* (1993). This story can be read as an allegory of the process of shadow and ego splitting and ultimate reintegration. For any unfamiliar with the tale it describes a young wizard who, in an outburst of arrogance, releases an evil being into the world. This then pursues him and he flees in terror, until he returns to his first teacher and learns that he must turn and face this shadow, despite his fear. He has to trust himself to chase that which he fears with no understanding of what will transpire.

I am doubtful that it is possible to deliberately seek our own shadow prior to that first encounter: it appears that this particular process has to be started from the inside before the journey can be taken up from the outside. I think of this as a double-locked door with one key being an intellectual acceptance of the concept of shadow, or some equivalent formulation, and the other being the felt experience of our own shadow. Without personal experience the concept is merely an idea that may fuel the mechanisms of projection and denial. Without conceptual understanding the felt experience may well simply result in a layer of guilt and remorse being placed on top of the other feelings involved. But when both keys are placed in the locks and the door opened then the threshold can be crossed and a conscious journey begin.

Once the door has been unlocked there are a number places in which it may be fruitful to search for clues as to what lies in our personal shadow. I intend to consider three such areas for exploration. The first comprises those projections where there is little or no relationship with the person being projected upon. The second is also a form of projection but is distinct in that it comprises projections where there is a significant degree of relationship with the person being projected upon. The third is in dream and fantasy images we generate which also offer an access point to shadow material. I will consider each in general and also from the particular perspective of the counsellor.

OBJECTS OF PROJECTION

When we project onto another person or group of people for us they cease to be human with volition and variety, we fix them in a particular form, sculptured objects rather than living beings. As such, they can serve some useful psychological function for us, but only if they remain in the position we have selected for them. As we employ this mechanism to deal with some of our personal shadow material it offers a means of identifying this process at work.

Distant objects

One of the areas to seek out evidence of our own shadow at work is to identify those people or groups of people towards whom we have a powerful emotional reaction, often disproportionate to the events involved. For example, I feel powerfully hostile to people who 'push in' in queues, not waiting their turn as I believe they should. My reaction is most marked when driving in lines of slow moving traffic that some seek to overtake. I feel self-righteously indignant, 'Don't they realise that their pushing in is what is slowing us all down so much?' These people become for me symbols of selfishness, of unfairness and I feel hugely frustrated in my inability to do anything to stop them getting in front of me. It is the intensity of these feelings that makes clear that this situation holds significant unconscious charge for me.

On the (of course very rare!) occasions when I overtake the slow moving traffic and push my way in further up the road I feel a strange mixture of shame and embarrassment (how did I get myself into this?) and delightful excitement. I can usually come up with some justification for my own behaviour: 'I've got boxed into this lane and it's difficult to pull over into the slower lane so I may as well go on now', or even better, 'I've got hungry/unhappy children in the car and I must get them home as soon as possible.' But the real tell-tale is the excitement: I want to jump the queue and take pleasure in so doing. The hostility I feel towards those other queue-jumping drivers I explain to myself as a response to their behaviour but truly it is my own primitive competitive hostility towards others expressing itself. My psychological process becomes even more transparent when taking into account the inhibition of feeling ashamed and embarrassed. This is almost certainly the mechanism I developed, presumably encouraged by those around me, in order to contain my rivalrous aggression. This can itself be further considered within a psychodynamic conceptual framework by considering my sibling relationships but that takes us beyond our current focus on the projection process.

For the process of projection to be effective it is important to be able to depersonalise those perceived to be the cause of the problem. Once one of those overtaking drivers is recognised as a worried parent, carrier of urgent medical aid, struggling businessman or confused octogenarian then they are no longer a satisfactory object for my projected hostility. They must remain faceless so that they can continue to be the heartless aggressor I cannot accept myself to be.

Asking the question 'What individuals or types of people do I have strong reactions toward?' is one possible way of gaining access to our own as yet unrecognised projections. As our shadow principally comprises those aspects of ourselves that we find unacceptable it is likely to be those people towards whom we have feelings that we characterise as negative. For the counsellor this exploration may be taken a step further by considering what patterns are discernible in our reactions to clients. We could consider whether there are certain types of clients, or particular presenting issues that fill us with a sense of dread. For example, if I generally feel critical when faced with someone who has a drug or alcohol dependency or despondent with depressed clients then this may reflect an unconscious aspect of myself being activated. What is more the client is being perceived as just that – a 'client' – with inevitable reluctance on my part to engage with this person in his or her own individual story.

Clearly there is a professional imperative to deal with such situations when the counsellor's feelings predominate the encounter as there is little opportunity for effective counselling to take place. However, our responses to clients may be quite subtle: little niggles rather than overriding feelings. The projection remains an obstacle to the counselling process but may not have a particularly obvious deleterious impact. If the projection is of this stereotyping form then it is likely to dissolve once we begin to form a relationship with the actual person who is the client. If we are to make use of this particular form of projection as a means of identifying our personal shadow it is in our first responses to clients that the clues are to be found.

An additional form of distant projection that we may engage in as counsellors comes about when we collude with the client in projecting onto some third party. When this occurs the client's partner, colleague, brother, mother, grandparent can become the reason for all their woes. As with most projections that stick, there is probably a grain of truth in this view, but it is part of our task to help the client distinguish between the grain and the whole granary. Once we enter into a collusive agreement any access to the client's shadow through this projective material is lost. It may also be a reflection of our own shadow that we are willing, perhaps eager, to enter this alliance. Identifying such collusive material is difficult and may well require the assistance of an insightful and sensitive supervisor. Nevertheless, it remains a valuable source of personal and therefore professional development.

Such collusion can be particularly seductive to us when we are working with client who has a similar experience to our own. As Lambers points out, 'The more fundamentally a (client's) problem is linked with the counsellor's personality, the less likely it is that he or she will be fully aware of what is being touched . . . ' (1993: 69). For example, the counsellor who had an aggressive and violent father may struggle to avoid collusion with a client with a similar paternal relationship. From a transference perspective this is a particularly alarming prospect for the counsellor. They may unconsciously recognise that if they challenge the client's wish to blame the client's father for all his or her current difficulties the counsellor runs the risk of becoming the object of all that anger. They will know the potential intensity of these feelings from their own experience and may balk at the prospect of having such feelings directed towards themselves. In such a situation the counsellor may well be understandably reluctant to consciously recognise the collusive process at work, for if they do so their professional integrity will demand that they address this painful area for themselves and consider challenging the client.

The counsellor may also fruitfully seek for projections in their views towards other counsellors. For example, Jane realised that she was harbouring suspicions that a number of colleagues were acting in malevolent ways towards their clients. She discussed her concerns with a trusted colleague who commented that either the local counselling community was in a dire state or these suspicions said more about Jane than all these other counsellors. Once she explored that possibility for herself Jane realised that she was troubled by the level of hostility and resentment she felt towards some of her clients. So it became apparent that Jane's suspicions were a projective manifestation of a denied aspect of her own shadow. Reflecting upon any such fantasies towards colleagues may again provide material that will assist us in the quest to learn more of our own shadow.

Close objects

When the object of projection is someone with whom I apparently have a close relationship there is a likelihood that the projection sets off an interaction between projector and object. This is quite a different process to when the object being projected upon is distant and therefore presumably relatively unaffected by this distant attention. There are many examples of this relationship-based type of projection to be found in a close-knit family, overlaying one upon another, sometimes developing very considerable emotional energy along the way. Emotional intensity is one of the distinguishing features of this type of interaction where there is a significant unconscious component. This is to be seen in the fiercely intense row between a couple who later will struggle to remember what the argument was supposedly about. It is as if they become combatants locked into a primitive fight in which words become ancient weapons with which they hack emotional lumps out of one another. There is little likelihood of unravelling such complex sets of interactions without assistance from one or more dispassionate third parties who must themselves be able to avoid becoming involved in a re-enactment of the battle (Hooper and Dryden 1991).

As a counsellor there is a rich opportunity to identify my shadow at work in the complex relationships that can develop in the consulting room. As the relationship with a particular client develops so the complexity of what may evolve increases. For it moves beyond the simple casting of the client into some stereotypical grouping I have devised that may occur when the client is still little known as a person. Gradually the client can become an actor in my unconscious drama just as I do for the client. Then I can usefully start to reflect upon my countertransference experience of the client in order to attempt to find evidence of my shadow.

I supervised a counsellor working with two clients who both had highly successful professional careers. I became aware that the counsellor, Giles, seemed to be using a lot of practical tools with both these clients: written exercises, relaxation techniques and guided fantasy. Giles agreed that he was using more practical aides than usual in his counselling. When explored further it emerged that he felt that it was important to do so otherwise these clients would not feel that they were getting value for money. Once Giles could accept this as his own projection – his fear that he had nothing to offer these successful people – he was able to return to his core client-centred approach. In the process of exploring this he was also able to acknowledge that he felt considerable disappointment in his own career progression and recognised that he was projecting his self-judgement onto these particular clients. However, his work with both clients continued to progress poorly. He and I explored the possibility that although we had uncovered a complex set of unconscious factors that he was working with in his personal therapy he had not, as yet, discovered the key to free up the therapeutic work. As there were two clients involved it was reasonable to assume that the blockage rested with Giles. At this stage he had not identified the shadow element which we both suspected was present.

We undertook a fantasy exercise in supervision that involved Giles imagining what he would say to one of these clients if he allowed himself to be really nasty. The ensuing vitriolic resentment was ferocious but led him to recognise intense feelings of rage and resentment. The historic focus for Giles was his father, who he felt could not stand him being successful because his father's own career had been dissatisfying and unsuccessful. Now we had the shadow involvement: this repressed hostility that was sabotaging the work with these clients. Following this the therapeutic work did start to progress. In due course Giles was able to make a number of brave and constructive decisions about his own career which were highly successful, not surprisingly now that the long-standing inhibition against success had been addressed.

THE SHADOW IN OUR DREAMS

In considering dreams as a source of shadow I include those that occur during physical sleep, those resulting from intentional image or fantasy work that is undertaken when awake (Ferrucci 1982; Whitmore 1991) and fantasies that arise spontaneously. There are significant differences of course in how these different forms of 'dreaming' occur and there may well be distinctions in the depth within the unconscious from which material is emerging. However, each is a potential source of shadow imagery that can offer a route to working with this material in creative and exploratory ways. To do so effectively does require a reasonably sophisticated understanding of our own dream world as there is a great deal of scope for misinterpretation such that the dream images simply become another set of objects to be projected upon. For anyone starting to explore dream imagery it is advisable to seek some assistance either from an experienced guide, typically a therapist versed in this field though some spiritual directors may also be appropriate, or through a dream group (Shohet 1985; Ullman and Zimmerman 1987).

When working with material that has its roots in the unconscious it is never possible to predetermine the nature of images that may emerge. Some years ago I had quite a fearful figure repeatedly appearing in my dreams. This character was in his fifties, some twenty years older than I was at the time, and in my dreams he was ruthless and violent towards myself and others. At the time this figure was stalking my dreams I had a frightening waking encounter with a stranger who, to me, strongly resembled this character. This I understood to be a projection onto this unknown person who simply bore some physical resemblance to my dream figure. In my struggle to accept and take ownership of this denied aspect of myself I drew extensively upon another dream figure: an old man. This second figure had been appearing in my dreams for some years and although somewhat fierce and demanding I understood him to be an ally: a mentor or teacher figure. In my personal therapy at the time the old man was a source of courage for me when addressing and starting to recognise myself in the first 50-year-old figure.

At the time all this was taking place, which was over a period of some months, I also had a most untypical private client who shared a number of alarming characteristics with this threatening dream figure. This client was a much larger and physically stronger man than I am and he appeared rather wild and manic due to prolonged use of a number of nonprescribed drugs. Although in his thirties he appeared much older, ravaged by the drug use and some years of sleeping rough. I was surprised that I held no fear of this client, feeling quite safe with him and warm towards him. Yet because of the personal work I was involved in at the time I was troubled by the possibility that I might be overriding my rightful caution of working with a client who could conceivably pose an actual physical threat to me. I was reassured by an appearance of the old teacher figure in a dream. In this particular dream I was troubled by shadow figures among some trees but he led me away and set me to the task of repairing children's sailing boats that were broken. He and I undertook this task for some time and then he urged me to go along a path leading from the inlet in which we were sailing the boats and not to let myself get further distracted upon the way. For a number of weeks I was experiencing this strange dichotomy, at times intensely fearful of a figure in my dreams and yet trusting of an actual man who might do me harm.

It took me some time to accept that the 50-year-old dream character was important for me but I was able to recognise that his ruthlessness and determination did indeed have a place if not allowed to go unchecked. I had to recognise my own potential to be vicious and cruel in a manner I still find unpalatable. As I did so I became (I believe) more able to exert a healthy form of authority and decisiveness that I consider to be the desirable qualities hidden within this seemingly nasty personage.

There are occasions when I include current or past clients in my dreams. There is no simple formula for determining what such an appearance may mean. The client figure may represent some aspect of myself or be a reminder of some other person in my life, but equally the client may be present as a way of reminding myself of something overlooked in my conscious reflections upon the work with this client. As an example I had a dream in which a client and I were on some sort of journey through woodlands. It was quite a difficult journey and I was anxious to reach our destination. Without warning a stag bore down upon us and gored my companion in the stomach, wounding him deeply. I then struggled to carry the now wounded client to find help and while doing this I awoke. In taking this to supervision I recognised some anxiety in my work with this client and a sense that I was trying to move our work to a conclusion. I interpreted the dream as a reminder of this and a challenge to myself to work with this client at a much deeper emotional (gut) level than I had been previously. In our next session, without any prompting from me, the client disclosed horrific abuse that he had experienced as a youth. This was a powerful example of self-supervision through the use of a dream image. It also, incidentally, typifies that curious phenomenon (observable from time to time) whereby the therapeutic work deepens following a supervision session in which new insight has been reached without any apparent bridging from the supervision by the counsellor. In my view such a dream appearance of a client does warrant careful scrutiny as it usually indicates that this particular client has some significance that is not being fully recognised. Only as the meaning is unravelled will it become clear whether such an occurrence belongs primarily in the territory of our supervision or personal therapy.

WAYS OF SEEKING OUR SHADOW

It is not easy to lift up the stones of which our daily life is constructed and look at what lurks beneath. Thankfully most of us have what Bollas has described as positive narcissism: '. . . an informed affection for ourselves so that the problematic parts of the self are confronted in a responsible and forgiving way rather than being subject to a merciless tirade. . . . this love . . . for ourselves is a continuous source of inner nourishment' (1991: 159). Nevertheless, it can be a disturbing process and there may be occasions when we utilise what we learn about ourselves in a more self-destructive manner. It is important when deciding to embark upon a deliberate process of seeking to discover what lies within our personal shadow to ensure that we have appropriate support and assistance in this work. As well as the support structures we have in our daily life it may well be important to seek additional help for periods of this journey. There are a number of forms such help can take.

Individual therapy

Undoubtedly, individual therapy can be one of the most effective ways of working with shadow material. At best it provides a safe environment where, as the client, we feel accepted and encouraged to take up the journey in a constructive and liberating way. Any therapist we work with will, of course, also have their own shadow so it is important to start out with a sense of trust in the practitioner we choose. Often being in therapy will catalyse more shadow material to emerge, as if the psyche recognises that this is an appropriate opportunity to do this work. This may happen within the therapeutic relationship itself, or through increased dream or fantasy activity. We may find ourselves working within the transference relationship with our therapist who then becomes the object of our projections. We may work with similar material in a very different way through examination of dream images, or guided or spontaneous fantasy images. What is important, whatever the style and approach of our therapist, is to be willing to face what emerges in whatever guise it arrives: to be willing to sit in the uncertainty that inevitably results from being the client ourselves.

As practitioners we are perhaps more likely than others to return to therapy a number of times during our life. As Johns puts it, 'there may be recurring moments of choice throughout professional life when a period of personal counselling will be valuable' (1997: 64). Given this it is as well to give some thought to what can be quite a costly undertaking, both financially and emotionally. I know that some continue to see the same therapist for many years, presumably because they feel this to be beneficial. It is certainly useful to have a substantial period with one therapist in order to work through the various levels in that relationship. However, staying with one therapist may become a cosy arrangement with little challenge or change. On the other hand moving from one therapist to another may simply be a device to avoid the deeper layers of psychological material that persistence will reach. A balance needs to be sought and a willingness to trust our own judgement as to when to persist and when to move on. While it is important for our professional competence for our initial therapy to be with a practitioner akin to our own therapeutic orientation, following this there is also room for more diversity. Indeed it may be that we want to include alternative health practitioners or spiritual directors in the range of people we consult.

Groups

Types of group that we might seek out or indeed find ourselves involved in include therapy groups, dream groups, personal development groups, peer support groups and brief workshops.

Therapy groups essentially have a similar brief to individual therapy but adopt a group-work approach (Whitaker 1985). In such a group the other participants are potential objects for projection so that a great deal more variations in projection become possible than with one individual therapist. However, the resultant complexity can be overwhelming or lead to much of the material not being sufficiently addressed. The effectiveness of the group will be greatly dependent upon both the skill of those facilitating and the mix of membership.

It is also possible to set up or join dream groups, using the approaches described, for example, by Shohet (1985). Such groups have a structure that is designed to limit the amount of intra-group projection and focus more on enabling each individual to explore their own dream material within a supportive context. Also, of course, a great deal can be learnt and our own unconscious stimulated by working with the dreams of other group members.

Many counselling training courses include a personal development group as part of the curriculum. While some question the usefulness of such groups (Irving and Williams 1996) they are widespread and potentially offer a supportive opportunity to process some of the intra-personal material that can be stimulated during the training process. In addition such groups 'also provide the trainee with the possibility of facilitating personal growth in other members of the group' (Connor 1994: 32). There is nevertheless a need for careful facilitation of such groups as the trainees will be in various stages of development and therefore variable in their capacity to provide effective support to one another. Even with professional facilitation the recognition of shadow material in such a group can be explosive and a destructive rather than constructive experience. When participants are starting to awaken their own dormant destructive potential this is more likely to emerge through enactment rather than as a carefully worded description. For example, those bringing to the fore their potential to be abusive or exploitative in a group that may also contain others who have themselves been abused or exploited are as likely to be pilloried and attacked as accepted and encouraged in their honesty. Yet if such potential is not recognised then it is far more likely to emerge in the practice of those trainee counsellors, with clients who are ill equipped to protect themselves from such harm. This type of group is one of a number of structures frequently offered to trainees, and often alongside review partnerships and keeping a journal (see p. 84).

Another type of group that may be a place in which shadow material can be examined is the experienced peer support group. This is a group in which the participants are experienced practitioners who, it is to be hoped and expected, have sufficient self-awareness and openness to be able to both support and challenge each other effectively. Such a group can be particularly valuable following individual therapy: it encourages us to take ownership of our own personal development while offering the containment of a knowledgeable group of practitioners. Certainly I greatly value what I discover about myself in the peer group of which I have been a member since 1990.

The brief workshop that is frequently on offer as a single event or as part of a conference is another form of group that can be helpful. Such workshops are rather uncontained and as such can leave the participant stirred up without the continuing support to make sense of what has occurred. Nevertheless, with an awareness of this drawback such events can be a valuable opportunity to work in an unusual way or with a facilitator who is able to draw out a particular aspect of shadow. Arguably such workshops are most valuable when embedded within a training course or for counsellors with a source of continuing support in which to take the new insights further.

Journals

For many centuries some people have kept a personal journal, or diary, for periods or throughout the whole of their literate life. This can be a simple diary or a more elaborate journal system such as that described by Progoff (1975). A journal provides a means of reflecting upon present experience and also of looking back both to review progress and to identify themes that may emerge at intervals over a given period. Often trainee counsellors are expected to keep such a journal or log. The usefulness can be undermined if the document is going to be read by others and assessed as course work, although the impact of this can be ameliorated to some extent by the use of clearly defined assessment criteria, such as those offered by Connor (1994). The learning journal does remain a useful device particularly during initial training when development is likely to be rapid and therefore difficult to process as it occurs.

In addition or as part of a general personal development journal it can be very helpful to keep a log of dreams, either continuously or for a period of a few weeks at a time. Often keeping such a log seems to result in the individual remembering more of their dreams than they would usually expect. Thus it can act as both an *aide-mémoire* and a stimulus to dream recall.

Personal creative work

Coltart suggests that 'in an ideal world, all psychotherapists would have a garden' (1993: 98). She makes this assertion in the context of the need for balance in our personal life with sufficient physical activity to counter the sedentary nature of our work. While I agree with this view I want to extend it somewhat further and suggest that creative activities such as gardening, cooking, drawing, painting, sculpture, needlework, writing and performing all provide a forum for significant personal development. This may be direct work on our shadow, for example using art mediums to represent aspects of ourselves that we cannot describe verbally. It may also be providing a creative context that helps to salve some of the aches or bruises that result from our encounters with troubled people. But generally being involved in a creative activity seems to open us up to the possibility of personal insight, perhaps because both are a function of 'non-dominant hemisphere brain' activities[2] although this is a somewhat speculative explanation. Silverstone in writing about her many years' experience as a person-centred art therapist suggests something similar when she writes, 'images, like dreams, tap into the world of spontaneous knowing, nothing to do with thoughts' (1997: 1). Similarly Lane (1991) talks of art as 'the language of the soul' that can move us beyond our more prosaic everyday consciousness to touch something of the mystery of human experience. For me it is important to be open to this other realm for myself and also for those clients who have experiences that transcend their usual understanding of themselves.

DEVELOPMENTAL IMPLICATIONS

There is a danger that this process of starting to deliberately seek out our shadow sounds rather bland and simple. In truth for myself and others I have witnessed during this period this is certainly not the case. Rather the conscious decision to start to do this work deliberately seems to often occur at the crescendo of a great deal of psychological activity, usually reflected in considerable change and upheaval in the person's life. We often only realise that this process is under way at a point when it has already reached such a momentum that it will not be stopped. Often the height of the crescendo is marked by a moment of recognition, a moment when we cease to attempt to flee the shadow that appears to chase us and instead turn and face what is there. Once this moment arrives it tends to herald a period of relative tranquillity, the eye at the centre of the storm, and for a while all can appear crystal clear and be viewed with great openness. The defences that were so heightened during flight still remain in place and are likely to slowly creep back into usage over the ensuing weeks and months. However, this hiatus does afford an opportunity for long-lasting change.

It needs to be recognised that moving through the stage of confrontation may be quite a bumpy experience. There may well be periods of intense excitement as insight and understanding emerges; however, there may also be periods of deep depression when it seems that all that has gone before is rather pointless and there is no way forward, no way out of the tunnel we find ourselves in. It can be hard to live through such a time and very hard to put on our counselling mask day after day and focus on our clients. Nevertheless we need to persevere and the discipline of doing so is itself a valuable, if exhausting, experience.

It is by no means inevitable that every person will come to a conscious recognition of their shadow in their daily life. It is another myth of the ego that consciousness is always necessary for growth and change to occur. But if we are to be effective counsellors we must be self-reflective, we must possess a conscious capacity to give meaning to our experience. It follows then that we must engage in this process knowingly, for how else will we be able to act as a guide to others endeavouring to tread this path? There may be moments when this feels too much as we look with envy at others who seem to move through life with relative ease and little apparent need to recognise their own psychological processes. At such times we can take some solace from the view that has been put forward that the more conscious approach is likely to result in a greater degree of self-development. In an attempt to provide just such comfort and encouragement Jacobi (1967) offers the analogy of the distinction between wild fruit and that which has been cultivated: the latter providing a much richer harvest. In truth the wild fruit are sometimes more tasty, but perhaps this just reflects the limitations of the analogy!

There may be considerable merging between the stage of confrontation and that of integration that follows. For quite a time we may struggle to face aspects of our shadow and then adjust to the consequences. While this is taking place the degree of attention and emotional energy available for work with clients is reduced. Provided it is recognised the experienced counsellor will have some capacity to manage this situation: they will know that they have less to offer than at other times. It is quite likely that they will have already dealt with previous periods of reduced effectiveness, for counsellors are not immune to the distressing times that occur in the lives of all of us (Norcross and Prochaska 1986). Indeed it is possible that as a group we are somewhat more prone to such experiences than the average non-counsellor (Henry 1966). Thus learning to continue to function with clients while in a troubled state ourselves is one of the skills we can all expect to have opportunities to call upon (Gold and Nemiah 1993). A counsellor with some ability in this area has resources if facing the onset of a major confrontation with their shadow.

The trainee or novice counsellor who is grappling with their shadow has no such previous experience to fall back on. They may well be oblivious to their poor level of focus upon the client, not seeing beyond their own self-preoccupation. Indeed the early stage of practice is generally characterised by an overly self-conscious attitude (Stoltenberg and Delworth 1987). Add to this the increased narcissism associated with a period of intense shadow work and the unwitting clients of the trainee are in a singularly vulnerable position. It is too glib simply to suggest that in such instances counselling practice should cease until the trainee is able to come through their intra-personal crisis to a more stable psychological state. There will be some occasions when this is an ethical imperative (BAC 1997) but many when it is not the chosen option. What is vital is that the containers described in Chapter 3 are effectively in place so that clients can be safeguarded. Then supervision provides a place where the quality of work can be monitored and decisions about stopping or restrictions on the range of client work can be made. For those counsellors whose shadow emerges at a crescendo of psychological activity there are particular dangers of clients being caught up in the confusion the counsellor will be experiencing. I shall return to this issue in Chapter 6.

Successfully negotiating the stage of confrontation affords us the potential to progress, as we gain in experience as a practitioner, through the developmental stages of exploration and integration that Skovolt and Rønnestad (1995) describe.

6 Incorporating the shadow

The task of bringing together the ego and the personal shadow begins with confrontation, facing those aspects of ourselves that have been denied because they have been adjudged unacceptable. This confrontation inevitably occurs from the ego: when I look at my shadow the 'I' with which I am identified at that moment is my ego and my shadow is 'other' to me. The desired outcome is one in which 'I' has been redefined to incorporate newly recognised aspects of the shadow into the ego in some new fusion or synthesis. This goes much further than a grudging acceptance as it involves the ego itself being transformed, which can only take place with the loss of the old ego. In reality while we continue to develop this is a continuing process with an increasing proportion of the shadow being made conscious. We do not reach a stage of complete synthesis: the relationship between our conscious and unconscious aspects is far too complex for that to be feasible. However, synthesis can remain the state we aspire to reach while this remains a useful way to direct ourselves forward.

The incorporation of shadow material into our ego is a daunting prospect, particularly at the outset when the shadow appears simply to consist of unpleasant and undesirable characteristics. That initial stage of looking into the mirror of the ego is vital and cannot be circumvented, however, once that has been done, once the unacceptable has been fully faced, then ways have to be found to bridge the gulf that inevitably lies between. The period of calm that can follow the decision to accept a particular aspect of our shadow soon dissipates as the tough questions about what to do with this new knowledge rise into awareness. Insight alone is not enough, it equips us merely for the role of guard, with the shadow remaining in the position of enemy attempting to infiltrate and cause harm. This is of course a considerable step forward from the previous state of ignorance but unceasing vigil is exhausting and doomed, eventually, to fail. To pursue the analogy, a way has to be found to move from the battleground to the negotiating table. Initial discussions will centre around finding a way to curb the worst excesses of each party and subsequently achieving a common way forward in which the best in each side is brought together.

To make this more concrete let us consider the example of a trainee counsellor, Joanne, who discovered that she has the capacity to feel intensely jealous. This emerged initially in her feelings towards certain other members of her peer supervision group on the counsellor training course she was undertaking. The intensity of these feelings frightened Joanne but she was able to acknowledge to herself that the feelings were real and started personal therapy in an attempt to make sense of what she was experiencing. In so doing she had taken the first step of facing this component of her shadow: she recognised a jealous aspect of herself even though it did not fit at all with her current self-image. The ensuing work with her therapist had a number of interlocking components that are typical of this process.

Initially Joanne needed to consider in detail the situation in which she experienced these feelings. This analysis led her to the view that she felt jealous when certain other members of the group were receiving what she perceived as positive attention from the facilitator. This she was able to link to her family experiences and in particular her jealous feelings towards her siblings when they were receiving attention from her mother. She was also encouraged to explore the shame she felt about this aspect of her personality, which at this stage was still very much 'other' to her self-identity. Shame has been defined by Fossum and Mason as '*an inner sense of being completely diminished or insufficient as a person. It is the self judging the self*' (1986: 5; original italics). The authors go on to distinguish between moments of shame that are acute episodes of intense feelings and pervasive shame that is a more chronic state linked to beliefs of self-worthlessness. Joanne was able to trace her own sense of shame back to a particular incident when in a moment of jealous rage she had pushed her brother off a slide and in falling he had broken his arm. She was then able conceptually to link the present experience with past events and relationships, thereby creating a working schema (Jacobs 1986). This achieved her first objective in going into therapy: it gave some context and meaning to what she was experiencing, unravelling a number of layers of feeling. Joanne found that this knowledge provided some reassurance, she was less frightened by the intensity of her feelings, and the intellectual structure enabled her to contain herself. Nevertheless, she still experienced this jealous aspect of herself as a foreign invasion, she did not feel it to be a part of who she was.

In order to proceed with this exploration it was necessary for Joanne to find a way to separate out the expression of these difficult feelings of jealousy from the enactment of violence. She struggled for some weeks with this difference for it felt to her that the expression and the action were inextricably intertwined. In an attempt to resolve this difficulty she did experiment with expressing the jealousy directly to those involved. She started this by acknowledging her feelings of jealousy within the relative safety of the counselling course where there were some at least who would support her in this endeavour. We need to remember that these feelings were emerging in a supervision group which had a clear focus upon the client work of the trainee counsellors involved. Perhaps a certain amount of time would be available for a personal development matter such as this but this would be tangential to the primary task of this group. In the event it was an importantly liberating experience for Joanne to say, on one occasion, how she felt and it did result in her having a more central role in the group from that day.

Joanne also recognised similar feelings of jealousy in situations with colleagues, friends and family members. However, her one attempt at direct expression in her family resulted in a sharp and hostile rebuke followed by a period of considerable awkwardness. Joanne's fear that expressing these feelings would make matters worse seemed well founded. This is a difficulty when working with feelings such as jealousy that are somewhat unpalatable to all concerned. Many do not have the relative safety of a counselling course group in which to attempt to give voice to that which has been repressed for so long. Yet there is an enormous subjective difference between describing a feeling in a dispassionate and detached manner and expressing the same feeling with some of the passion and emotion it arouses. Nevertheless, expressing feelings such as jealousy, envy or hatred to those towards whom the feelings are directed is often problematic. Indeed it is generally wise to urge caution and deliberation if someone is considering doing so as the consequences may be considerable. Joanne learnt this lesson the hard way, for it took some time for family relationships to recover equilibrium following her expression of jealousy.

There are a range of techniques available for expressing emotions directly through catharsis (Heron 1990) in the safety of the counselling setting. Such catharsis can be very valuable: it provides a route by which the hitherto repressed emotion can be fully experienced and released. Once we have really felt our fear, anger or grief coursing through our body this experience changes us in some way. It is as if a channel has been opened which in future situations will be available to be put to use again, usually in a less dramatic and all-consuming manner. However, cathartic techniques are generally most applicable to singular expressible emotional forms such as anger, sadness or fear (or indeed happiness or joy). The feeling components within a particular shadow characteristic tend to be somewhat more complex and therefore do not always readily lend themselves to cathartic release. Attempting to express a feeling such as jealousy, which is an emotional cocktail, through catharsis can be somewhat disturbing and disorienting and as such counterproductive. Nevertheless, when shadow material is emerging into consciousness it is important to find some way to bring it fully into the light.

For complex emotional states, one effective approach is to use fantasy as a means to access what the shadow, if completely unfettered, wishes to do. Such fantasies will often be quite violent and dreadful but provided it is very clear that considering the fantasy is not an invitation to enact these wishes this is not in itself problematic. Indeed to experience the fantasy and the accompanying feelings provides not only an opportunity for this experience in itself but also the reassurance of being able to contain the desires and trust our own sense of judgement as to what is acceptable behaviour. I recall some years ago that I was pushing my daughter in her buggy when a youth on his bicycle almost ran straight into her. My instant, and imagined, desire was to rip this poor young man's head from his body. I suspect my quietly spoken 'please be careful' was uttered with great intensity. It was an immense relief to formulate the intense feelings that surged through me into that gory image, that I had not the least intention of enacting. This then is the distinction between the fantasy and the action that it is so important to establish in order for shadow material to be explored in reasonable safety for all involved.

If fantasy is used it is important that it does not become an end in itself, it would become highly counterproductive to simply stay within such an image or indeed to start to use it in a gratifying way. The fantasy is essentially a bridge, a means to traverse the dangerous waters that lie between insight and integration. As such it is not to be particularly lingered over but rather used as a means of making progress. It is not essential to create a florid image such as the one I offered but it is important that the individual finds some way to experience the shadow characteristic. For some this will occur naturally as the recognition takes place but for others this may not be sufficient as it may remain a distanced intellectual awareness. Using fantasy is but one of the options for accessing this feeling material directly. The use of artwork (Dalley 1989), dramatic reconstruction (Badaines 1988), or the various *Gestalt* techniques (Clarkson 1989) are all therapeutic alternatives. Each offers a different experiential way into the shadow material.

Returning to Joanne, once she had given voice to her jealousy she was able to move on to the next stage. This involved separating out the various levels of feelings that were running through her that she had initially experienced as one single thread. With assistance from her therapist Joanne was able to recognise that her desire to be violent was a reaction to the mixture of pain and loneliness that welled up within her when others received the affection and attention she yearned. Thus she learnt to drop beneath the initially violent response and feel this underlying hurt. In this way Joanne ceased to be frightened by the intensity of her rage and in so doing drew the teeth of this aspect of her shadow. Unlike her jealous feelings the pain and distress that emerged was far more amenable to cathartic release, it had a more primary emotional nature. Much of this cathartic work took place in the sessions with her therapist, where the safety and privacy was a great asset.

Some way through this process Joanne was struck by the irony of her struggle to accept this jealous part of herself, given her commitment to the values of counselling. For central to the basis of counselling is the acceptance of the person for the whole of who they are. Curiously, although perhaps not surprisingly, Joanne was viewed by her peers as being a particularly empathic and accepting counsellor. What is more, she was an advocate of the desirability of speaking one's mind honestly even though this may bruise the sensibilities of those being spoken to. Thus there was a very clear split between the expectations and values Joanne held for her clients and those that she had been imposing upon herself. This could be taken a stage further. The discrepancy lies between the values Joanne consciously espouses as an adult and those she unwittingly took on during her upbringing: the values residing in her shadow. This surfacing of her values was another important part of this process for these unconsciously held values are as much a part of the shadow as the feelings and thoughts. While these values remain unconscious they could continue to exert a powerful influence upon Joanne: an undertow acting against the movement towards incorporation.

By this stage Joanne has travelled a considerable distance from the original intense feelings of jealousy that first alerted her to the need to enter therapy. She has identified the shame she felt about her jealousy and she has been able to explore the injunctions from her parents about not expressing strong emotions that fed this sense of shame. She has gone on to work directly with the pain and loneliness that inhabited the core of the jealous component of her shadow. This has left her with a much clearer view of the emotional landscape lying behind the feeling of jealousy. What had previously been simply a turbulent and overwhelming internal experience now has a form to it which is comprehensible. When Joanne feels jealous she is now able to give some meaning to this experience. She can recognise that this feeling indicates her desire for some of the attention someone else is receiving. It is possible to use this as an internal communication to herself, a signal, to behave in a way that results in her receiving more attention. In the supervision group, for example, this may mean saying what she is thinking about the work currently being presented. This is a far more productive and task-appropriate response than simply bemoaning her feelings of jealousy towards the other students. Similarly in work or social settings it may mean taking a much more active role than has been typical for Joanne. These each represent positive ways of using the energy from her shadow and getting her own needs met in an acceptable manner.

This inevitably involves a major perceptual shift: the individual needs to step back from the sense of repugnance for this aspect of themselves and find some productive means of harnessing the essence of the feelings involved. We have used the example of jealousy but this is but one of the powerful and seemingly destructive feelings that may inhabit the shadow. The challenge may be to make use of aggression or hostility, finding a means of utilising the powerful raw energy involved without attacking or causing pain (Storr 1968). Harder still perhaps to find a means to transform hatred, the desire to sexually dominate and humiliate, or a cruel and vindictive aspect of personality. Yet such is the challenge that results from confronting our shadow.

It is arguably part of the function of the counsellor or therapist to remain optimistic about such a task even though it may at first sight seem virtually impossible to achieve. In psychological terms this amalgamating the shadow with the ego is not a single event but rather a process. Joanne will not preclude her potential for jealousy with her first attempts to articulate and then transform the feeling. What she will be achieving, and this will continue for many months and years, is a gradual reduction in the potency of this aspect of her shadow. If the contents of the shadow are brought into the light of day and every effort made to make use of the essence rather than express the raw form then the shadow will become smaller, and therefore have less influence in the person's daily life. This is the hope that we can rightly hold for our client, and this can only be done with surety when we have ourselves undertaken this task.

Something else occurs that assists in this process once it has begun. The psychic energy[1] that has been used to contain this aspect of the shadow is no longer required and is therefore released. It is as if there has been a battle going on behind the scenes, with the shadow attempting to escape and the ego maintaining its incarceration. Once a truce is agreed then both sides can release the resources, or psychic energy that have been taken up in the conflict. This generally results in an increased sense of vigour and enthusiasm that can be further utilised in this task, and is also a boost in itself.

IMPACT UPON CLIENTS

It is apparent from the example of Joanne that the emergence and movement towards incorporation of an aspect of personal shadow can result in a
particularly chaotic period in the individual's internal life, as I have already
suggested. Joanne lived through a number a months of volatility in her
day-to-day emotional state and her underlying mood. She would move
from intense anger through to periods of calm, days when she wanted to
curl up and cry and others when she felt raw and exposed, times when she
felt excited by the progress she was making and others when it felt hopeless
and never-ending. It only gradually became possible for her to recognise
the sources and stimuli to her feelings as they were occurring. As this
happened so it became possible for Joanne to work with the feelings by
identifying the underlying needs and seeking legitimate satisfaction.

When Joanne first recognised the level of her jealousy within her
supervision group she was already seeing a number of counselling clients.
Throughout these turbulent months Joanne was active as a counsellor
and she falls into the category of trainee counsellors I alluded to at the
end of Chapter 5. She had only been counselling for a few months and was
undoubtedly very much at the novice[2] or first stage as described by
Stoltenberg and Delworth (1987). This left her without any substantial
internal reference points as a counsellor once she started to engage with her
jealousy. As a consequence she struggled to make any sense of her affective
experience when she was with her clients. She had little or no basis for
making assessments as to what were simply feelings she brought with her
into the room, what was her own material being stimulated by the client
and when her feelings were a reflection of syntonic countertransference.
Alongside this difficulty clients inevitably experienced Joanne as quite
volatile in her mood and her actions. This was understandably problematic
for some of her clients and it is never possible to ensure that this is not so.
Considerable attention was paid to this in supervision and Joanne was
encouraged to be watchful for such 'fallout' from the therapeutic work she
was herself undergoing.

In general it can be anticipated that some clients will be adversely
affected by a counsellor in such a process and this may not always be recognised or dealt with. These are often the clients who need the consistency
from the counsellor that was lacking in their early experience: those for
whom the counselling relationship is what Clarkson (1990) describes as
reparative or developmentally needed. If consistency is not experienced in
such a therapeutic relationship the results can be disturbing and counterproductive. This cannot be avoided or glossed over for the basis of this kind
of therapeutic work is founded on the principle of providing a 'secure frame'

(Langs 1982). Bowlby writes that: 'The therapist strives to be reliable, attentive and sympathetically responsive to his patients' explorations' (1988: 140). It is unrealistic to expect a counsellor who is in a variable state to be reliable or constant for their clients. The counsellor may consider themselves to be calm and collected when with each client but any such assertion probably contains a degree of wishful thinking.

It is equally the case that some clients may benefit from this process of change that Joanne is moving through. It relates to what it is like for the client to experience the counsellor in a range of emotional and psychic states as she moves along this journey. For some clients this may be quite liberating and encouraging as they are metaphorically pulled along in their counsellor's slipstream. They are able to recognise the humanity of their counsellor and take courage from the struggles they recognise this other person is willing to go through. This is a form of what Buber described as the 'I–You' relationship (1970), where the client and therapist meet at a human level of authenticity that transcends the formal roles of the therapeutic encounter. However, as Clarkson rightly points out: 'Genuine well-judged use of the I–You relationship is probably one of the most difficult forms of therapeutic relating' (1990: 155). The inexperienced practitioner such as Joanne is unlikely to have the degree of therapeutic sophistication required to instigate knowingly this form of therapeutic engagement. The best we can realistically hope for is fortuitous or intuitive I–You contact that the client is nevertheless able to utilise.

During this period Joanne has been strongly discouraged by her supervisor and tutors from making any deliberate changes in her behaviour towards clients. There are a number of reasons why this is important. At a level of general principle it would be inappropriate, indeed almost certainly unethical (Bond 1993), to make any such alteration, for at this stage Joanne is essentially involved in an experiment, behaving in a manner that is significantly different to her traditional response. It is readily understood that to use clients as subjects in a formal research experiment without their permission would be wholly unacceptable (BAC 1997). For a while Joanne is involved in an informal experiment and as such the same proscription has some bearing. What is more she will inevitably be far too involved in her own subjective experience to be able to effectively monitor the impact of this new behaviour upon those around her. It will take some time for her to accommodate this change within herself and be able to recognise her effect upon others.

This proscription against deliberately experimenting with new behaviours towards clients does afford some measure of containment of the turbulence Joanne is experiencing. However, it would be very naive to believe that there will be no disruption in her therapeutic relationships simply because

Joanne has agreed not to consciously experiment with new behaviours towards clients. As she moves through her own personal therapeutic process so she will change in subtle ways that will inevitably alter how she relates to others, including her clients. Changes such as these cannot be contained or excluded from Joanne's therapeutic work because they permeate aspects of all her relationships.

Supervising counsellors or therapists who are going through periods of rapid personal change such as that described for Joanne can be very challenging. For the supervisor has to try to assess the potential impact upon the clients whilst not undermining the developmental process at work in the supervisee. This can only be done collaboratively, the supervising and counsellor working together in this task. When I have been in this position I have sometimes offered an image of the counsellor in a boat travelling down a very fast-flowing and turbulent stretch of river. If the clients are thought of as being towed, each in their own craft, behind the counsellor's boat then we can think about which of the clients may be vulnerable to being capsized. Attention can then be paid to how best to assist each client, with a range of options available to be considered. It may be appropriate to talk to some clients about this part of the river. For Joanne this might mean alluding to the fact that she is going through some personal discoveries and that she may be somewhat volatile for a while. Such a level of disclosure needs to be considered very carefully but some clients with whom Joanne has a strong 'working alliance' (Dryden 1989) may find this useful information, allowing them to monitor the situation for themselves. There may be ways of steering some clients into shallower water, focusing on therapeutic goals and tasks that are very different to those Joanne is grappling with for herself. This is quite a legitimate therapeutic strategy provided that the goals and tasks are ones the client is committed to undertaking. The final option of cutting the rope, i.e. severing the therapeutic work, remains a possibility. However, this should be the last resort to be used only if the client is felt to be at risk of being harmed should the counselling continue, as cutting the rope is irreversible and may in itself be quite damaging. Sometimes a short period of sabbatical is possible without the clients being permanently lost.

Our focus on the example of Joanne has meant that we have been concerned with the situation when the shadow emerges in a setting outside of counselling itself. However, there are occasions when the shadow first emerges with a client as was the case for Sally who was working with a client who had discovered she was pregnant. The client, in some distress, was describing how she had been persuaded into having sex at a party and hadn't thought about contraception. Sally was horrified to hear herself say, 'Well, really what did you expect?' Her client looked shocked and Sally was herself dumbfounded. She quickly apologised and tried to assure her client that she hadn't meant what she said. When the session was finished Sally quickly made an appointment for supervision. Initially she and her supervisor wanted to believe that this was some form of countertransference but there was little evidence to support this proposition. Sally did go on to explore her own beliefs about sexual behaviour and realised that despite her own espoused liberal attitudes she had heard her mother and grandmother talking very critically of girls and young women who had become pregnant outside marriage. She had to recognise that such views also existed within her despite her very different consciously-held beliefs. When something like this occurs the starting-point is often particularly messy as the shadow has already caused considerable pain and confusion. It is particularly important in such a situation to focus on the relationship with that particular client and assess what may assist to heal any hurt that has been caused. It is also essential to reflect upon the remaining clients the counsellor is seeing, who may be vulnerable to similar treatment.

The difficulty of increased narcissism has been considered as a general phenomenon that may detract from the attention and awareness the counsellor has available for the client. The counsellor is then suffering from what Heron describes as having 'dull antennae' or simply 'absent awareness' (1990). However, there is another aspect of narcissism that also needs to be guarded against. There is a tendency that I have observed in myself and others that when an individual is consciously focused upon a particular aspect of psychic material they perceive this particular phenomenon everywhere. When attention is, for example, upon the potential to envy then everyone seems to be expressing envious tendencies in one form or another. This is very simply understandable as a consequence of the temporarily heightened awareness of this particular aspect of human experience. Indeed it may be that this overemphasis is an important part of the process of embedding this new awareness into consciousness. However, it does mean that many, if not all, the clients of a counsellor going through this phase will have their envious tendencies scrutinised regardless of whether this is of any great relevance to them at that moment. This unfortunate tendency results in the counsellor hijacking the agenda, determining quite a narrow focus for the work for awhile. For some clients this may be a salutary challenge but for others it is likely to be an irritating distraction from what is central to their concerns at that time. Again it is unlikely that the counsellor will notice this taking place, being too heavily immersed in the process. Once more it will fall upon the supervisor, or perhaps astute colleagues, to alert the counsellor to this danger and encourage its avoidance. It does usually wear off after a while but it is an interference in the client's work and as such should be avoided if possible.

There is another phenomenon that is observable during the period of shadow integration, a phenomenon which can be thought of as a 'potency disparity'. When we start to become aware of and start to experiment with a new-found aspect of ourselves we tend to feel very tentative in the attempts. We tend to experience ourselves as cautious and uncertain in our actions, often still raw and vulnerable from the experience of baring our soul, if only to ourselves. Yet the counsellor who is experiencing him or herself in this manner will often seem very powerful and possibly alarming to their clients. If this disparity is not understood and due allowance not made in therapeutic interactions clients may well leave sessions feeling somewhat laid bare. Once again this is rendered more dangerous because the counsellor is usually unaware that it is occurring, being preoccupied with their own self-consciousness. Applying this to Joanne I am proposing that when she first starts to integrate her jealous side there would be a considerable discrepancy between how she feels and how her clients experience her. When trying to be more expressive she would feel anxious and vulnerable but her clients would generally perceive her as increasingly powerful. This effect is not restricted to interactions with clients, it is likely that some of Joanne's colleagues, friends and family would also find her new-found directness quite alarming and intimidating.

A particular example of this danger is what I think of as 'post workshop syndrome'. This occurs when a practitioner goes on a training workshop that particularly touches them and awakens them in an intense way to a particular aspect of themselves. Typically such workshops occur at weekends and the clients who have appointments on Monday morning may be in for an alarming session. An intense experiential workshop can leave the counsellor in what amounts to an altered state of consciousness for a period of a few days, gradually dissipating as the week progresses. This is particularly likely when there has been a dramatic experience of release for the counsellor during the workshop, with the increased psychic energy particularly marked for the next few days. If this energy is utilised without being moderated it can pierce defences that the client may not yet be ready to let down. In my view workshop facilitators need to be meticulous in pointing out to participants that some period of recovery may be required and that for those particularly affected a few days without client work may be advisable, if not essential. If nothing else such a warning should make the practitioner more alert to their predicament.

These represent a sample of ways in which clients may be affected when a counsellor is undergoing a period of intense personal development. Clearly it is unrealistic to expect counsellors to be unchanging year on year, indeed it would hardly be the role model we would like to offer clients who seek counselling precisely because they wish to make changes in their lives.

Nevertheless, such times of intense psychological change within the counsellor are of a different order or magnitude to the changes in state that result from the vagaries of life that we all encounter. A considerable degree of watchfulness at such times is the responsible and professional response. This monitoring needs to be done not only by the counsellor but also by their supervisor and when relevant those involved in their training.

DEVELOPMENTAL IMPLICATIONS

As it becomes possible to accept and indeed embrace aspects of the shadow which hitherto have been unrecognised, or perceived as a dangerous enemy to be guarded against, so a change within the perceptual or cognitive framework takes place. The nature of what is understood as 'I' by the individual has changed. 'I' is no longer wholly identified with the ego but has a rather broader base. One manifestation of this that some demonstrate is represented in a shift in perceptual model: no longer is there a view of this being good and that being bad. Similarly it is recognised that 'there are not, as the world thinks weak persons on the one hand, and on the other the strong' (Tournier 1963: 176). Rather there is a sense of middle ground existing upon which apparent opposites – good and bad, weak and strong, ego and shadow – can and do coexist.

One of the arenas in which this may appear for counselling practitioners is that of self-assessments[3] (Heron 1989). These are often required both during training courses and as part of the portfolio of work presented for professional recognition and accreditation. Reflecting on self-assessments that I have undertaken during my own training and professional development the early ones often seemed to fit into the polarities of strengths and weaknesses. However, as I have gained in experience this has shifted, such that in later assessments, each issue I focus upon tends to be described in terms of appropriate balance, with the polar extremes being decried. I have noticed a similar shift in the self-assessments others have written over a period of time. It is to be hoped that this change of perception will move beyond the narrow confines of self-image and inform and influence practice.

Once we have really embarked upon the process of facing and incorporating our shadow then we are actively involved in our own personal and professional development. Provided this process continues and does not become blocked, as can happen, then we can expect to continue to deepen our capacity to work well with clients. Within the framework offered by Skovolt and Rønnestad (1995) we are likely to be in, or approaching, the stage of individuation. They use this term to describe the development of the counsellor as a creative practitioner with our own individual style based upon experience as much as original training. It is perhaps not surprising that they have used the same term as Jung (1959a) uses to describe the process of psychological maturation. As we do start to move into this phase of our development as practitioners so it becomes possible for the sixth and final stage of the process I am describing to occur, the shadow acting as a guide to the therapeutic work.

7 Shadow as guide

As we come to know our shadow better so we become less fearful of what it contains. As we become less fearful of our shadow's potential to do harm in our work so we become less suspicious of our responses to clients. As we become less suspicious of our responses so we become more willing to utilise those responses in our therapeutic work (Wosket (1999). As we become more willing to use our responses the distinction between ourselves as a counsellor and ourselves as a person diminishes. This process is reflected by Skovolt and Rønnestad as they describe how 'the individual gradually sheds elements of the professional role that are incompatible with one's own personality and cognitive schema' (1995: 109). This is, and needs to be, a gradual process, taking place over many years. It will sometimes accelerate when we take a risk with a particular client and see how it pays off. Equally there will sometimes be setbacks when we say or do something that we later realise was inappropriate and undermining of our work with that client.

We do need to continue to scrutinise and consider the possible source of our thoughts, feelings, fantasies and the actions that may result. Done effectively this is not a glib interpretative process but rather a thorough self-questioning, much in the manner described by Casement (1985) as 'internal supervision'. At the same time we do not want to relate to clients in a stilted or passive manner. There will be times when we are suspicious about the source of a particular response to a client and then we do need to reflect and perhaps have discussion with our supervisor. Nevertheless, I would suggest that ideally we are aiming to be able to interact with clients in a direct and lively way while simultaneously monitoring what we are doing. This is very demanding and I usually have some clients where I fall well short of this. I suspect that with these individuals I can seem rather formal and perhaps distant but I prefer that to my reacting in ways that I do not trust. With such clients I continue to aspire to being immediate and free-flowing in our interactions and my capacity to do so becomes one of my measures of the effectiveness of our work together.

When I defined shadow in the introduction I proposed an initial model with the shadow as a specific aspect of the larger personal unconscious characterised by the potential to be destructive (see Figure 1, p. 0). I now want to reconsider that model somewhat because I believe that the most useful way of thinking about the shadow changes as our relationship with ourselves changes. That initial definition was consistent with not knowing a great deal of the contents of our personal shadow. It encourages us to face the real destructive potential we contain, which is itself an important step in the recognition and confrontation of our shadow. At the stage we have now reached in the process of shadow incorporation that dualistic way of distinguishing constructive from destructive, 'good' from 'bad', becomes increasingly redundant as it is superseded by an understanding based much more on the concept of balance. We recognise that the unconscious aspects of ourselves have the potential to be creative and inspirational as well as destructive. Given this, the boundaries between the potentially destructive shadow and other elements within the personal unconscious blur and are often inconsequential.

INCUBATING OUR RESPONSES

Sedgwick has described a countertransference model in which the therapist is deliberately receptive to their own thoughts, feelings and fantasies while with the client. This is allowed to deepen and the therapist deliberately focuses upon these responses within themselves. There may be interpretation back to the client but there is an alternative in which the therapist goes through a process of 'incubation' (Sedgwick 1994). In this way the thought, feeling or fantasy is allowed to influence the therapeutic process in an unspoken manner. I recall counselling a young woman, Pauline, and finding myself feeling increasingly protective towards her. I felt that she was quite vulnerable and I admired the way she faced her difficulties in what I considered to be a very courageous manner. What I also recognised was that the feelings I had towards Pauline were similar to those I have had, on occasions, towards my daughter Hannah (6 or 7 years old at the time). I focused upon these feelings towards Hannah and as I did so I remembered a number of times when I had felt this way. Each was an instance when she was doing something new and independent: going to stay overnight with friends, going on a school trip and starting Brownies. Rather than spend time during the session wondering why I was having these feelings towards Pauline I assumed that I was making an unconscious link between Pauline and Hannah: as if the father in me was trying to tell the counsellor in me something important about Pauline. I was able to offer something of this back to Pauline in an interpretation recognising the desire she had had when younger for her father to protect her from her mother's emotional tirades. What I also recognised from my own experience as a father was that the moment for protection was past. Pauline did not need me to be protective but rather she needed me to communicate my trust in her capacity to look after herself. I did not articulate this directly but it did influence the perspective from which I offered my interventions from then on. The protective fatherly aspect of me is not intrinsically destructive, far from it. I understand it to be that powerful instinctive urge to protect progeny recognisable among parents throughout the animal kingdom. However, had I unknowingly acted from this protective instinct I might well have done a disservice to Pauline by undermining her rather fragile, yet trustworthy, sense of autonomy.

The model Sedgwick proposes is rooted in an analytic formulation for therapeutic relationship; nevertheless, it offers a paradigm for all practitioners. It challenges us to understand our own experiences while with a client as a significant aspect of the therapeutic field of which we are both a part. What matters is not the source but that when we have reached this stage in our development we are no longer frozen by the fear that what emerges may be from our shadow and counterproductive for the client. We have enough confidence in our ability to distinguish between our harmful and helpful desires that we can allow our unconscious thoughts, feelings, and fantasies to enter the therapeutic field, trusting ourselves to spot if we are getting drawn into something destructive. There remain risks in so doing but a certain degree of calculated risk has always been the hallmark of therapeutic practice that aspires, and at times reaches, beyond the mediocre.

WITNESSING UNCONSCIOUS PROCESS

I have had the experience of working with clients when I have been aware that I did not consciously understand what was happening even though there has been every indicator that progress is being made. I am not referring to the short-term confusion I regularly experience at stages in my work with many clients. Rather I am thinking of that quite rare occurrence of having a deep sense throughout the therapeutic relationship of being involved in something beyond my conscious grasp. One way of understanding this experience is that the client and I are involved in a therapeutic process at an unconscious level. At its most extreme this can feel like my unconscious is doing the therapeutic work while my conscious self idles away the sessions in harmless chatter with the client's conscious self. This may just be some grandiose delusion on my part and in some instances probably is but it seems to me useful to allow the possibility that such an unconscious process may be at work.

I am reminded of the work I did with a particular client who I shall call Alan. He was an intelligent and attractive man who seemed to have everything going for him. He was very successful in his career, was in a long-term sexual relationship, had many friends and was involved in a range of activities that he seemed to enjoy. Yet he was deeply unhappy. Not depressed according to clinical criteria but deeply and consistently unhappy. He felt guilty about this, very much aware that he had everything and therefore 'should be very satisfied, and grateful'. We explored many different areas of his life: his current relationships, work, family, early years and experiences at school, beliefs and values. I felt that we had an easy, comfortable relationship and looked forward to our sessions. At the same time I had a lingering uneasy feeling that we were never really touching the heart of Alan's difficulties.

At one stage he was involved in a new task within his job and finding it very hard. He struggled to prepare to a level he felt was sufficient and continually felt out of control of the process, although all the feedback he received suggested that others were very satisfied with his performance. I suspect that in part at least my own unease stemmed from a parallel sense of lack of control – I didn't know where I was trying to go in my work with Alan. Then after many months of little outward sign of progress, Alan started to make changes. He took time off from his work, separated from his partner and started to get involved in voluntary work to which he felt highly committed. He started to appear different, gone was the sheepish and slightly hounded look as he faced the world much more head-on. He continued to make progress and in time brought our therapeutic relationship to an end, expressing gratitude for my part in the changes he had made. This may sound like a very straightforward and effective piece of counselling work and for Alan it would appear that it was. But throughout our relationship I could not, and as I write about it now still cannot, shrug off the pervasive sense of having being involved in a process that, at some fundamental level, I do not understand. It is as if I know that something deeper was occurring between us, which I believe was therapeutic for Alan, but remains out of reach of my comprehension.

In one way what I describe with Alan is not unusual. In my current work in a university counselling service it is common to see clients for just a few sessions and to observe remarkable progress that I know I play little or no significant part in. My role then is to be the witness, the one who hears and perhaps simply holds the knowledge with the client of what they are living through. But with Alan I remain convinced that our work was central to the changes that transpired while being unable to explain satisfactorily the considerable gulf between what I have consciously been involved in and the healing I perceive to have taken place. This is not a unique example in my experience. It is somewhat akin to what Ferenczi, writing in 1915, described as 'Dialogues of the Unconscious'. This term is used when 'the unconscious of two people completely understand themselves and each other, without the remotest conception of this on the part of the consciousness of either' (Ferenczi quoted in Bollas 1995: 10–11). The difference between what Ferenczi describes and my experience is that I do consciously have a remote conception at least that something was occurring unconsciously, although I cannot articulate what that was.

This idea creates such an opening for self-deception that I introduce it with some trepidation but without it we deny the healing potential of our unconscious. We grasp at elements of this potential in those 'mistakes' whereby hindsight tells us that we played a significant part in the constructive therapeutic outcome, but this can be thought of as occurring despite our actions or dismissed as mere good fortune. What I am proposing is a more positive view of the effect of our unconscious whereby it may be considered, on occasions, to facilitate healing separate from our conscious interactions with the client. This conclusion can only be arrived at by interpretation and is open to much challenge; nevertheless I suggest that we do well to make allowance for the possibility.

ATTENDING TO DETAIL

One way to allow our shadow to guide us is by noticing the details of what takes place, those minutiae we may well overlook completely or be inclined to dismiss. The introduction opened with an example of this, with the detail being the subtle discrepancy, the slight sense of incongruity, between the intended meaning of the words I spoke and the flavour of the tone in which I said them. Other examples include noticing the client it takes longer than usual to recollect in the morning when I see just their first name in the diary: what does this tell me about how I feel towards them? The client I think about on my way home and the fantasy I almost have about them but then don't allow to form in my imagination: where might it have taken me if I had? The offhand remark in supervision as I move on to talk about another client: what might we find in this remark if my supervisor and I stop to ponder it? The twinge of physical sensations, not sufficient to call pain but nevertheless noticeable, that I sometimes have part way through sessions with a particular client: does that relate to this client having multiple sclerosis or does it have some other meaning? When

I have to take a couple of days off because of a sudden brief illness and I feel guilty about a particular client having their session postponed: what does this tell me about my view of this client or my relationship with them? The client I am particularly eager to see: what am I getting from our relationship?

These are just a few examples of the clues emerging from unconsciousness that may assist us to a deeper understanding in our therapeutic work. We notice them by being on the lookout for such information and by being more curious than anxious about what is in our shadow. There are also less subtle events that it is hard not to notice, such as the client we double book, call by the wrong name, feature in a powerful fantasy or forget a crucial piece of information about. In these instances it is then a matter of our attitude towards what we observe. By this stage in our development it would be hoped that most times we are open and curious, reverting rarely to defensive or anxious self-conscious responses.

To consider a specific example I have a client in whose presence I frequently have the same fantasy. In this set of images I am trying to devise ways to build a rustic lodge in a woodland area. This is not a fantasy I have any other time and it has no direct association, that I know of, for myself or this client. The main reason that he comes to counselling is that he finds it helpful to have somewhere to talk about what is taking place in a difficult and demanding relationship he is in. The interpretation I put on my fantasy is that it is a reminder to me of my purpose for this client: I believe that I offer him a haven to which he can retreat when the need arises. There is something soothing for me about the imagery and I suspect that it encourages me to relax into serving the purpose I have described and letting go of any need I may have for a more tangible or finite therapeutic goal.

FOLLOWING 'INTUITION'

Another way in which we may be guided by our shadow is in the form of intuitions or hunches. The term 'intuition' can be understood in a number of ways, I am using it to describe the phenomenon of having a strong sense of knowing something without any conscious basis for that 'knowledge'. There are probably a number of different mechanisms that result in these 'intuitive' experiences in a counselling relationship. We may simply be having a recollection of something to which the client has previously alluded but we do not consciously remember. It may be that we are putting together a range of disparate pieces of information or clues to identify an overall pattern without being aware that this is what we are doing. It may reflect some symbolic understanding that we are not able to explain in rational language. At their deepest levels such symbols can offer a way forward through opposing psychological forces as they represent 'the third factor or position that does not exist in logic but provides a perspective from which a synthesis of the opposing elements can be made' (Samuels *et al.* 1986: 145). An intuition may also be some form of communication between ourselves and the client that takes place outside of consciousness. We might be most comfortable thinking of such communication in terms of unconscious processes already described, such as projective identification or transference. Alternatively we may prefer to think in terms of deep empathy or indeed some type of parapsychological occurrence. Whatever the means by which a hunch arises and how we understand it to have come about there are important questions that need to be addressed.

One question we need to consider is: 'Does this intuition have a ring of truth about it?' which is a way of reflecting upon the likely trustworthiness of the hunch I have. Another way to address this is by asking myself: 'Does the intuition have a sense of rightness?' when I sit with it for a while. This is important because of course we can take any feeling or idea we have about the client, which may be no more than projection or simple stereotyping, and dress it up for ourselves as an insightful intuition. If, after some reflection, we conclude that we do trust a particular intuition then the next question is: 'What, if anything, do I do with it?' This is a delicate matter as offering a hunch in its raw form or at the wrong time can be very alarming and disruptive for the client. A relatively common example is the client who assures us how perfectly idyllic their childhood was when we have a strong sense that this is far from the case. We don't know for certain but our experience, or hunch, tells us that what they are presenting indicates that they have probably been the subject of significant levels of emotionally or psychologically damaging parenting. We may have a clear idea of what actually did take place or just have a general feeling of the incongruity between what we are being told and what we are observing. We then face the choice of containing our response and waiting to see if an opening emerges, or indeed the client reaches the same view as we now have, or finding some way to challenge them. How we proceed will need to take account of our assessment of the current strength of the therapeutic relationship as this is an important factor in the likely usefulness of direct confrontation. There is also an option of using the incubation approach described earlier (see p. 102) to see how our understanding about who the client is and what they are living develops in the light of our intuition about them.

WORKING FROM OUR OWN WOUNDS

There are times when meeting a client involves us working from what Sedgwick (1994), and before him Jung (1966), has described as the wounded healer archetype. The mythological exemplar of this archetype is Chiron (or sometimes Cheiron), the immortal centaur who was a renowned teacher and healer but suffered unceasing pain resulting from a wound to his foot. A more detailed account of this story can be found in Graves (1960). The challenge for counsellors is to find a way for our own wounds to inform and enrich our work while in no way taking away from the focus upon the client. It only becomes possible to start to rise to this challenge, or even comprehend it in any depth, when the wounds are recognised, explored and sufficiently integrated to no longer form a threat. But this willingness to open our own wounds in the encounter with a client is not to be scorned or seen as an unfortunate necessity. It helps us to develop a degree of humility, the ingredient that separates true compassion from mere pity. Those who practice in this field without humility are in danger of taking up an omnipotent position as a therapist. If this happens then we are going down the path of losing touch with the basic human equality which is the hallmark of any truly helping relationship (Kopp 1974; Brandon 1976; Dass and Gorman 1985).

The most profound wound that I have had to contend with in myself is a deep and unsatisfiable loneliness. It is only in recent years that I have developed the capacity to use this to good effect in my work. In my early adult years this wound was a dangerous aspect of my shadow that drew me into inappropriate relationships in which I tried to meet this unconsciously driven need with little understanding of the emotional demands I put on others in the process. After one particularly difficult personal relationship I started to recognise something of what was happening and determined to confront what I was doing by choosing to live alone for awhile. I recall thinking that unless I could sort out my relationship with myself I would never be able to form a satisfying relationship with anyone else. This became an important turning point as I then had to face my loneliness with no-one else to hide behind.

At this stage I was usually able to contain my loneliness when working with clients although from time to time it did leak out. On a few such occasions I suddenly found myself trying to say something encouraging and supportive to a client and realised that my words made little sense to me. It was as if I suddenly 'awoke', feeling very embarrassed, to be met by a somewhat quizzical look from the client. I was able, with the help of some sensitive supervision, to start unravelling this process and uncover the loneliness I was feeling but was trying to mask through my inappropriate comments. It then became possible to identify that I felt this way with clients who were themselves vulnerable to feeling very lonely. From there it became possible to start developing the ability to recognise and use my loneliness as a measure of the client's own feelings. This happened in parallel with the work I was doing on this wound in my personal therapy.

Since that time there have been a number of occasions when my own sense of loneliness has been the first evidence that a particular client is struggling with a similar feeling. As my confidence in this process has grown, I have been increasingly willing to name this loneliness for clients, a number of whom have been very relieved that I have been able to do this on their behalf. It seems that the loneliness to which I am sensitive is intertwined with a feeling of shame that makes it hard to speak of these feelings. In recent years my own loneliness has become less intense as a consequence of the healing that has taken place through my own therapy. It has further reduced since I have established a satisfying personal relationship and my partner and I have started a family. Despite this there are still times when the loneliness I experience with a client is very sharp and I have to overcome my reluctance to having these feelings.

The potential pain of working in areas close to our own wounds should not be underestimated. A wound is raw and vulnerable and when the salty tears of a client fall upon it the pain may be too intense to bear. It is to be hoped that work in personal therapy will lessen the degree of pain but for many of us there will remain areas in which our own vulnerability will continue to be restimulated by clients. What characterises the counsellor able to operate from the wounded healer within is the conscious capacity to feel our own pain and stay present both with this pain and with the client. It is a truism that all counsellors are human and therefore have their own wounded suffering aspects, but I am proposing an actual emotional reality, not merely an intellectual construct.

I hope from this it becomes clear that in my view the process of increasing shadow incorporation, which can result in the shadow being a guide rather than merely an unwelcome passenger, is not one of becoming impervious, or of dealing with all personal history to such a degree that our own suffering can no longer be touched by the suffering of others. Rather, it makes it possible to be able to stay consciously vulnerable and not slide off behind the defences of unconsciousness once more. When we have our own pain touched by the client and are able to use this constructively in our work with that client this is one clue that the valuable potential of our personal shadow is being utilised. There is a second clue that can also be drawn from the experience I have described; the anxiety I still feel that my own process might get in the way of my work with the client. It is a particular form of anxiety, a recognition of being on a knife edge and while having a sense of trust in what is occurring remaining aware that the therapeutic nature of the process is quite precarious. This quality of intermingled anxiety and trust is quite different from the rigid certainty that characterises denial or delusion. Another way of describing this is to say that when we are afraid that our shadow might be involved yet are honestly not able to give any evidence to back up our fear, then this may indicate that we are being guided by our shadow. It is reminiscent of the notion that one of the important indicators of sanity is the fear that we may be going mad.

ASSETS IN THE SHADOW

Throughout I have emphasised the destructive potential of the shadow side because it is my view that as counsellors it is these aspects that we must address first if we are to fulfil with integrity the task we undertake. I want to offer some measure of balance to this by acknowledging that our personal shadow also contains elements of ourselves that are potentially highly constructive and creative. We can easily place into our shadow some of our greatest gifts, perhaps not knowing what else to do at the time. Take for example the child who has the capacity for great acts of selfless generosity. They may well realise that such acts show up a rather more mean-minded parent or sibling for who they are. One way to deal with this conflict is for the child to deny their altruistic tendency so that all around can be rather more comfortable. Similarly as counsellors we are often too ready to dismiss our commitment to the people we try to help and our understanding of the self-serving side to our motivation may further encourage us to do so. In the Service where I counsel we were once thanked by a senior member of the organisation for our 'devoted work'. At first I, and my colleagues, felt very embarrassed to have such words used and wanted to dismiss them. We were all very reluctant to acknowledge any devotion to our work, this was not something we recognised in ourselves. Then I watched what we were doing, and I saw counsellors who were determinedly trying to do their utmost for clients. I saw reception staff working through most of their lunch break during a busy period in order to keep on top of the administration necessary for the Service to perform its task. I acknowledged the persistence with which I was pursuing local mental health workers to ensure they responded effectively to a person who I felt was in urgent need of their intervention. I could criticise all this for over-involvement or poor workload management but I preferred, somewhat sheepishly, to accept that perhaps there was indeed some evidence of devotion to our work. In as much as I, and my colleagues, did not recognise myself as 'devoted' to my work this is a simple example of an asset in my shadow.

Talking about the 'gold in the shadow' Johnson suggests: that 'People are as frightened of their capacity for nobility as of their darkest sides. If you find the gold in someone he will resist it to the last ounce of his strength' (1991: 45–6). This fits with the experience that I have when running workshops on the shadow. One of the exercises I sometimes use is to ask participants to think of someone they really dislike or detest and then take a few minutes to describe the attributes of this person to a partner. I then ask them to think of someone they really admire or look up to and again describe this person's attributes. The key to this exercise is to encourage participants to identify those individuals towards whom they have a powerfully energetic reaction. Later they are invited to consider the possibility that the attributes they have described, both negative and positive, represent some aspect of themselves and reflect upon how they might be different if these characteristics were manifest in their daily lives. A significant proportion of participants, in some groups the majority, struggle more to accept the positive attributes originally ascribed to the person they admire than the negative ones identified with the person they dislike. I suspect that this is typical of a general reluctance that many of us have to identify and take ownership of those capacities and gifts that we are not at present realising. To do so demands a particular form of courage, for once we accept that we have certain strengths we have also to decide in what ways, if any, we shall put them to use. While we remain in the relative comfort of mediocrity no such sense of responsibility arises. I suspect that there is another important reason why we resist acknowledging our noble aspects, that is when we open the door to allow a gift to emerge from our shadow we are also very vulnerable to other potentially destructive characteristics finding their way out. If this is the case then it follows that the more we know and can contain our destructive tendencies the more likely we are to be able to free our hidden attributes.

One of the other ways of observing the 'gold' in our shadow is to notice what we are capable of doing in unexpected moments of crisis. There are often examples in the news of individuals who display great courage at a time of peril. The person who rushes into the burning building, the one who instinctively tries to help the stranger putting their own safety at risk – or the person who faces up to a threat that logic suggests they cannot match. Similarly many of us will have been tested in less dramatic circumstances, do we bend down and comfort the person who has collapsed in the street or do we feel embarrassed and walk past rationalising that others are better qualified to offer help? And if we stop, are we able to learn from this and overcome embarrassment in other circumstances to reach out to those who seem to be in need? For it is often easier to react instinctively in the moment than it is to apply this same courage in a measured way.

Assets in the role shadow

Alongside aspects of ourselves we are not realising in any part of our lives there may also be elements of who we are that we express and are comfortable with in some areas of our lives but restrict when we are involved in counselling work. I have already suggested that we may be able to gradually allow such characteristics out of the role shadow and into the counselling room with us. It is also worth considering a bolder attitude that proposes that these aspects of our personality may be essential assets in our full therapeutic repertoire.

One aspect of myself that I put in this category is my bluntness, which sometimes leads me to describe events or situations as I see them without the tact or sensitivity I prefer to display towards clients. I find being blunt in other areas of my life refreshing at times but I remain uncomfortable about acting in this way when counselling. Intellectually I know that being blunt can be an effective form of confrontation provided that it is offered with a loving, rather than punitive, intent. What I experience as bluntness in me is, I think, the uncompromising aspect of what Heron describes when he talks of confrontation needing to be 'on the razor edge between love and power, and be both supportive and uncompromising' (1990: 45). I suspect that on occasions bluntness achieves success where a more carefully crafted response may not. However, knowing all this does not take away my sense of discomfort when blunt with clients. I do not like the shock it can cause and I feel somewhat out of control when I speak to clients in this way.

One example of this occurred when a client was describing, in a rather joking tone, how they were behind with their academic work and ended by saying 'It isn't very good really is it?' to which I replied 'No, it sounds like you are in a right mess.' Hardly a textbook example of empathic paraphrasing but my response did seem to encourage them to take their predicament seriously. They went on to make, and carry through, effective decisions about how to limit the damage. Another example, which had potentially more dangerous repercussions, involved a client who had recently returned after a spell in a psychiatric hospital for what he described as a psychotic episode. This was the third or fourth such episode in eighteen months and yet he seemed almost complacent about his condition, keen to forget about it and return to what he described as his normal life. I was very concerned as he seemed to have little understanding of the potential seriousness of his condition. Furthermore, in the past each time that he started to feel better he had stopped taking medication and this was the prelude to the next episode. Having ascertained that no-one had explained to him what might happen if this cycle continued to recur, I told him that in my view it was important that he did what he could to minimise the number of episodes as cumulatively they might cause him some degree of permanent psychological damage. Rationally I considered what I said to be a very cautious and measured way of describing the possible long-term effects of repeated psychotic episodes. Nevertheless, he was horrified by what I said and I was alarmed by his response, fearing that he would become very dejected and lose motivation as a consequence. When he came back the next week he told me that he had been angry with me for what I had said but went on, in great distress, to explain that for a long time he had feared that he was really going mad and had not dared to ask anyone if this was the case. I was able to reassure him that I was not suggesting this (as I was confident that my concern for possible psychological damage did not accord with his notion of being mad) but felt he needed to know what was at stake. He was able to describe his fear that he would end up in the awful state of some of the people he had seen in hospital who had been described to him as burnt-out schizophrenics. Over the coming weeks I admired the courage with which he started to face an uncertain future, accept that he needed to take his condition more seriously and indeed develop strategies to minimise the likelihood of further episodes.

I am not advocating this kind of bluntness as a deliberate intervention as its impact is highly unpredictable and it can easily backfire. It may be that other less direct interventions could have had the same effect. However, I suspect that this is not always the case and that my somewhat impulsive human responses usefully assisted the therapeutic process. As you will gather, this aspect of me remains in my role shadow as I write: I am still not reconciled with being blunt as a counsellor. The discomfort I feel is the indicator of this being role shadow material. I have reached the stage when I recognise that this aspect of my personality can be useful in the role. I am reasonably sure that my acute level of discomfort in such situations is disproportionate to the actual bluntness with which I have spoken, but I have yet to fully confront what underlies my discomfort and until I do this I suspect these feelings will continue.

This example of my bluntness is just one of the potential assets that may lie in a counsellor's role shadow. Others might include impatience, jealousy, envy, pessimism, cynicism, a tendency to tease, unrealistic idealism, a desire to gossip or to be the centre of attention. These are just a few examples because what I am proposing is that *any* aspect of our personalities that seems incompatible with the role of counsellor can, with care, be found a purposeful and constructive place in the consulting room.

When we are able to recognise the truth of this and put it into practice then we know that we have indeed travelled a considerable distance along the road of incorporating our personal shadow.

REFLECTIONS

In a way we have come full circle since the explorations in Chapter 1 of how the shadow comes into existence. For example, when I started to explore the shadow for counsellors I raised questions about the apparently laudable motives that we believe bring us into the work. I do believe that it is important to do this as it is one way of looking beneath the defence that can form a protection against knowing ourselves more fully. Now we return to the point when it is important to accept again the gifts and abilities we possess in order to utilise these gifts fully in our work as counsellors. These gifts may well be part of what brought us into this field in the first place. This is one example of a more general circularity that permeates personal and professional development. When we start out as counsellors we learn a different way of being and relating, yet over years of practice the gap between the professional persona and the self diminishes to become imperceptible. As opposites within our psyche are integrated so we move towards a greater 'wholeness' (Samuels *et al.* 1986). This is not a static or fixed psychological condition but rather is one dynamic possibility that occurs from time to time before we move on to confront other hidden aspects of ourselves.

Alongside the circular movement there is a linear progression as we move through the shadow incorporation process. I have noticed how my focus changes as I think about the different stages. At the outset I am concerned about containment and anxious about the dangers that the counsellor's shadow poses to clients. But gradually this shifts and I want to be more expansive, feeling that it is increasingly important to take risks rather than play safe. For me this reflects the process I am describing: as we become more familiar with our shadow so it becomes a more accessible and increasingly valuable aspect of who we are. We move from being rightly fearful to being increasingly respectful of little used aspects of ourselves.

I have now reached the end of the six-stage process that I introduced in Chapter 2. The final two chapters spread my focus out from the individual counsellor in their role to encompass first the client and then the broader professional context within which counselling takes place.

8 The client: mask, person and shadow

When someone decides to seek out counselling this is presumably because they anticipate that it will be helpful in some way. Often a new client is not particularly clear about what they want from counselling or indeed how it will assist. Nevertheless they expect that it will result in some gain, some improvement in their quality of life. It is my belief that in the majority of instances this is the case, that counselling is indeed a productive experience for the client. I imagine that most of the time all in the profession will share this belief. If counselling were not, on balance, living up to this aspiration then it would not attract and hold the many committed people who work in the field. All practitioners will inevitably have those occasional days when all the evidence seems to refute this belief, the client whose carefully nurtured progress crumbles and falls away, those who never arrive for the sessions booked or seem to give up on the therapeutic work, others who decide against committing themselves to the tasks that seem so necessary and urgent to the counsellor. But the times when there are more than one or two such disappointments are thankfully rare and easily forgotten in the face of more positive results with others.

SHADOW ASPECTS OF BEING A CLIENT

For the client the shadow side of the counselling experience manifests itself in the true failures. These are the pieces of counselling work that, when the reckoning is complete, amount to a negative experience, with the client emerging from counselling in a worse state than when they entered. This does not mean temporarily distressed or troubled but rather it means being significantly diminished in some way. Examples of this include an inability to function, a decreased sense of self-worth, an inability to deal with emotional experience, less trusting, more fearful, more depressed or more despairing. The frequency of this is quite difficult to quantify because research into counselling outcome tends to average results and so hide individual failures. Nevertheless there is no doubt that sometimes counselling does fail and the client is left to deal with the consequences. There are examples where clients are unlucky enough to be subjected to ineffective or even incompetent counselling and yet seem able to learn and develop through the experience. Allen (1990) provides a lucid example of this in her description of being the client of two quite different counsellors. She is in no doubt that the counsellors were not helpful to her and yet her account suggests that she has been able to extract useful lessons and insights from the experience. However, this is serendipitous: clients can reasonably expect useful results because of counselling, not despite it. To use an analogy from the game of cricket it is quite common for a bad delivery to get the batsman out but woe betide the bowler who believes that this means they can get away with bad bowling. Just as it is the bowler's task to bowl their best so it is our responsibility as practitioners to make every reasonable effort to perform our craft to our utmost ability by 'simply doing impeccable work' (Kopp 1977: 13). Part of that, I propose, is to be alert to ways in which we might unwittingly contribute to causing harm rather than being of assistance.

I suspect that when we think of clients for whom counselling is a detrimental experience we tend to wonder what their counsellor did wrong. In many cases counselling is harmful because of some action, or inaction, by the counsellor. This I have already explored in some depth when considering the shadow of the counsellor. I now want to consider another possibility which is not as common but nevertheless can result in counselling being a disservice to clients. I am referring to those occasions when harm results from the intrinsic nature of counselling itself. I think of this as the potential shadow of counselling itself that can have consequences for being in the role of client.

I am suggesting that the essential components that constitute the particular type of human interaction that we term counselling have their own shadow side. In order to support this proposition I intend to examine a number of elements of counselling and consider examples of the shadow side of each. I shall explore the following:

- The belief that change is always possible which can lead to a false sense of hope.
- The eventual betrayal inherent in counselling.
- Unrecognised influence hidden behind the intention to assist clients to find their own solutions.

I also want to consider the following shadow possibilities:

- Counselling can have seemingly legitimate therapeutic consequences that the client does not want.
- Talking can sometimes be counterproductive.
- Being a client can stigmatise the person.

It is not inevitable that harm will result from any of these and an astute client assisted by a wise counsellor can probably successfully negotiate all such pitfalls. However, I am proposing that these dangers do exist, that the unwary client can fall foul of them and that when this does happen the source of the danger lies in the shadow side of the function of counselling rather than the personal shadow of either participant.

False hope

It is undoubtedly one of the functions of counsellors to maintain an optimistic perspective for our clients: to be a source of hopefulness. The realisation that we believe in the client and their potential is sometimes the crucial ingredient in effective therapeutic work. This can instil again a sense of hope in the client and enable them to find the courage to start acting on the premise that good things could start happening. It may also make it possible for some clients to dare to sink down into the pit of despair that they circle around yet are loath to enter, fearing that they will never emerge again. The therapeutic potency of this hope, this optimism, must not be underestimated. Yet it is also possible for this same optimism, that can be so vital, to be quite destructive for particular clients. This may seem unduly harsh language to use but I think not, for when hopes are raised that cannot be fulfilled the effect is likely to confirm the client's despair. Indeed it may further add to the level of desperation for a possible solution has been lost, perhaps counselling is the latest in a long line of resources that have been tried without success.

The time where we can most easily fall into the trap of engendering false hope in clients is at the beginning of our relationship. In my view we have a responsibility to make an effective assessment, with the client, about the nature of the difficulties that bring them to counselling. Included in this needs to be a recognition that the fact that someone has come to see us does not ensure that counselling is the most appropriate help for them at that time. There may be difficulties that need to be dealt with in other ways. Take the example of Trevor who had been experiencing bouts of severe depression since his early adolescence that were apparently not brought on by any external events or stimuli. He had never had any medical or psychiatric assessment but had 'muddled through' and was presenting for counselling because he felt it was becoming increasingly difficult to cope. In starting to talk to Trevor it became clear that he was detached from any emotional experience, other than this pervasive depression, and that he had a low stress tolerance. It was also apparent that he did not have any sense of being able to engage with his difficulties. He made it clear that he wanted some relief, someone to take away the torment he was experiencing. After the initial two sessions I told Trevor that I wanted to refer him for a psychiatric assessment in order to get a measure of his depression. I continued to see him for a few weeks in a supportive capacity, and he was eventually diagnosed with a moderate degree of endogenous clinical depression[1] and responded very well to medication. He was immensely relieved and eager to get on with enjoying his new-found sense of well-being, so we brought our work to an end.

In my view it is important for a client with a potentially serious psychiatric condition, such as Trevor, to seek the psychiatric assistance they require just as it is important for a client with a potentially serious physical condition to seek medical help. Also I consider it to be my responsibility to ensure that I do not collude with a client who has a serious psychiatric difficulty by allowing them to believe that counselling will provide the answer to all their needs. To do so would be creating false hope and be setting the client up for later disappointment. As Lemma, writing about psychopathology from a counselling perspective, puts it: 'It is, however, clear that not everyone is inclined to talk about their problems nor that such an intervention brings about the change, for instance in mood or anxiety, that the client desires' (1996: 52). I do not intend to imply that counselling has nothing to offer someone with serious psychiatric difficulties. However, I view it as only one component in a co-ordinated approach that needs to include appropriate medical monitoring. Considering counselling clients with serious psychiatric or physical conditions Daines *et al.* suggest that: 'Particularly with psychotic states and serious physical illness there may not be benefit to be gained [sic] from working with a person in a way that undermines their psychological defences and increases their awareness of their underlying psychological state' (1997: 15). It remains a point of contention as to whether undermining the psychological defences of clients with psychotic symptoms can cause harm rather than simply result in no benefit.

There are other issues of suitability as not all potential clients are actually ready to become active participants in a counselling process. Ruddell and Curwen offer three simple questions that can help to clarify this, asking to what extent does the client 'acknowledge the problem? recognise her own contribution to the difficulties? demonstrate motivation?' (1997: 79). Some clients may be able to generate active, rather than passive, responses to these questions but others may be so wedded to their own sense of helplessness that counselling is doomed to failure.

It is not easy to make the assessment judgements I am proposing but I do believe that we need to make the attempt. This will occasionally mean rejecting someone who presents themselves for counselling. How much more pleasant it is to agree to see each person who arrives, convincing our-selves that everyone is able to accrue some benefit from counselling. While I have some sympathy with this view at a philosophical level, in practice it remains my belief that counselling is not always the most appropriate form of assistance for an individual at any given time. Furthermore, as counsellors we do have more information about counselling and other forms of help than most clients. It follows that we have some responsibility to ensure that the client is able to make an 'informed decision' (Widiger and Rorer 1984) when entering counselling. In my view it also falls to us to be clear if we truly feel that counselling is unlikely to be useful. To continue under such circumstances would be disingenuous and difficult to justify from an ethical perspective.

Assessment does not stop at the question of suitability of counselling in general, for it must also consider the appropriateness of the particular form of counselling being offered. Dryden, when replying to an article entitled 'Do Therapists Ever Cure Clients?' (Rowan 1994), says: 'I do agree that the therapist can't do the work for the client, but she does need to take responsibility to provide the client with the right tools' (Dryden 1994: 9). While I suspect that, given our different therapeutic backgrounds, I would not always agree with the tools Dryden would choose for a client, I do, however, agree that as counsellors we have a responsibility to assess the suitability of what we offer to the needs of the client. If we do not have the necessary tools then we should be clear about referring the client else-where. By tools I mean the repertoire of skills to work with the specific issues the client presents. In my own practice I usually refer on clients with serious psychiatric conditions and also those who I believe will most benefit from a cognitive-behavioural approach that I cannot offer. It can be tempting to work with a client in areas outside our competence if they are reluctant to see someone else but this is unlikely to have a satisfactory outcome for anyone involved and is specifically proscribed in the BAC *Code of Ethics and Practice for Counsellors* (1997).

The assessment of the suitability of what is being offered concerns the counselling structure as well as the approach or skills base of the counsellor. Some may benefit from long-term psychotherapeutic work but simply be left high and dry by a relatively brief counselling experience. There is, for example, a considerable risk of disappointment if a highly needy and vulnerable client is encouraged to emotionally engage with a warm and caring counsellor who is only able to offer a six-session contract. In con-sidering the suitability of clients for brief counselling Dryden and Feltham summarise the indicators of the likely success of short-term counselling 'whether your clients have well-defined concerns and goals. Consider what stage of change they are at – whether they have had good enough relationships previously (as a sign that they can relate to you) – and what social supports they have' (1992: 22–3). Clients not meeting most of these criteria are probably going to accrue little benefit from short-term work and are better referred for longer-term counselling. By the same token some who meet these criteria may benefit more from the clarity of working on specific goals in a brief focused format than they would from the more diffuse process usually found in longer-term work.

In some instances it is undoubtedly the case that a client arrives and proceeds to invest the counsellor, and the counselling process, with unrealistic hopes of utter transformation. When such fantasies can be held and contained within an effective therapeutic alliance (Greenson 1967) then this may become valuable material for the therapeutic work. However, there will be occasions when such hopes go unrecognised and ultimately result in the client feeling that they have been let down. This sense of disappointment may be important, as it may be a necessary step in the acceptance by the client that their desires cannot be met, rooted as they are in unsatisfactory previous experiences. Without insight alongside such feelings, however, the counselling relationship will probably be merely experienced as an unpleasant re-enactment of other, usually childhood, relationships. It is often not easy to know how we are being viewed by a particular client: what unrealistic expectations are being invested in us. If as counsellor we have played some part in raising these hopes without subsequently working them through with the client then a breach of trust has occurred. Whether or not trust has been broken, if the client emerges further disappointed with no more insight into their predicament then the overall effect of counselling has, at this point, been negative.

Betrayal

The relationship between counsellor and client does require a certain degree of trust, and where this is lacking it often becomes the first area that needs to be addressed. However, this is not a simple matter, for as Hillman so succinctly puts it, 'Trust has in it the seed of betrayal' (1990: 278). When the counselling relationship is established it may well be that we are already heading towards betraying the client. This may come about as an unintentional act by the counsellor that has the effect of betraying. I worked with one adult client who came to me at a time when her personal relationships were in a chaotic state. Some months into our work I was invited to lead a very attractive piece of training, but it was on the day I usually saw this client. We discussed a possible move to another day and she appeared to be quite amenable and relaxed with this proposed change. However, once it happened she became increasingly emotionally inaccessible and despite exploring her sense of being let down by me, a few weeks later withdrew from counselling. While I have no way of knowing for certain I interpreted her termination as a direct consequence of her experience of being betrayed by me in my act of changing our appointment day. With hindsight I consider that my mistake in this example was in misreading the stability of our working alliance. I had thought it reasonably solid but I suspect that it was not, given that this relatively minor form of betrayal was, seemingly, irrecoverable. This particular example can be thought of as coming about as the result of my shadow. It suited me to change the day so I may well have ignored clues that moving the day of our session would not be tolerable for this client at that stage in our work.

It is also possible that the client will feel betrayed by events that are beyond the conscious control of all of us. We may fall ill, or indeed die (Kaplan and Rothman 1986; Alexander *et al.* 1989; Trayner and Clarkson 1992), our contract of employment may come to an end or we may be made redundant, become pregnant (Bridges and Smith 1988; Rosenthall 1990) or have to take a break from counselling because of stress or personal difficulties such as a divorce (Pappas 1989). The reality is that we are human and therefore subject to unpredictable circumstances that can interfere with our work with clients. In some situations it is possible to work through this kind of occurrence and for some clients a sudden interruption or cessation of counselling may be a spur to new growth, but for other clients such an experience will be very difficult and painful, a further betrayal or abandonment. How well an individual client is able to deal with such an occurrence will, at least in part, reflect how able and willing they are to see past any fantasy relationship they may have with the counsellor and recognise the person in the role.

There is another form of betrayal possible that results from offering this unusual form of relationship. It is the betrayal inherent in the qualities necessary for effective counselling, qualities that any of us may long for: acceptance, warmth, interest, an undemanding presence and an opportunity to discuss deep concerns with encouragement and without interruption. At best all this is experienced by the client in counselling on a regular predictable basis. But it will also be withdrawn at some stage for counselling is, by definition, finite. Many clients are able to utilise this opportunity and move on with their own personal friendships and support network picking up needs no longer being met when counselling ends. However, there are some clients who are left bereft after counselling, grieving for a way of relating, or a specific relationship, that is no longer available to them.

Ward writing about her pain resulting from therapy ending makes the important point that: 'Unfortunately for us clients, we are not designed to have intimate relationships on such a casual basis as is sometimes experienced in therapy. Therapists get used to this weird, unnatural arrangement and cope much better' (1998: 15). There lies an important warning in her words, for as practitioners we may indeed get used to the paradox of the intimacy that we hope does occur in counselling alongside the inevitable ending that will take place. For those left grieving as a result this is a particularly unpalatable form of betrayal.

Unrecognised influence

In a review of the literature on what clients report as finding helpful about counselling McLeod (1990) points out that receiving advice is one of the most highly valued factors. Along with this goes a concomitant dissatisfaction when advice is not forthcoming, this being seen as unhelpful or uncaring. Yet among counsellors it is axiomatic that counselling does not involve giving advice. This is instilled at the outset of many introductory courses and remains one of the defining characteristics of the activity of counselling (BAC 1997). The reason for this is linked to the principle of autonomy: it is believed that offering the client advice is likely to undermine their autonomy and may foster an unproductive form of dependency. Heron (1990) does acknowledge that advising, or prescribing what the client should do, plays a legitimate part in the helping role but I suspect that for many counsellors this notion remains uncomfortable. We are left with the paradox that this activity that is consistently valued so highly by clients is, purportedly, anathema to the practitioners. Such a major divergence, a split, inevitably forms a favourable breeding ground for shadow material.

It is only possible to speculate as to the cause of this difference for, as McLeod (1990) goes on to point out, there is little research evidence to clarify the situation. It could be that counsellors are, in selective instances, giving advice while decrying this generally as an appropriate strategy. This has some legitimacy for it is generally more honest and simpler to offer advice rather than use tangential interventions that contain the advice as veiled suggestion. At least when the counsellor's opinion, for that is in essence all that advice can ever be, is without disguise it is usually more visible for what it is.

An additional possibility is that clients are interpreting as advice what the counsellor genuinely intends to be facilitative. Indeed to take this idea to the extreme it might be that counsellors are reflecting back what is being said with such deft skill that the client takes their own words as sound advice, but this is a highly optimistic interpretation. Nevertheless many of us will have had the rather alarming experience of being thanked, or perhaps criticised, for telling the client what to do when no such directive was intended. This may result from the client using us as a form of authoritative alter ego thereby giving themselves the permission they need in order to act as they wish. But unless we are aware that this is taking place the whole process is somewhat out of control. The client's desired course of action can just as easily be self-destructive as self-enhancing. As counsellors we are often not aware of how we are influencing decisions that the client is making, even though it has been recognised for a considerable time that counselling does involve the counsellor exerting influence upon the client (Strong 1968). It may be that we need to recognise that despite our honest efforts not to be a benign (or malign) autocrat there will be times when the client and the role combine to force us into this position. This is an aspect of the potential power of the counsellor that we must not ignore, power that we may, as Shohet (1992) points out, like more than we like to admit.

There is another form of influence that the counsellor can unwittingly exert, not through any particular harmful intent but simply because each of us is also a human being with our own particular life experiences. I offered the example of the different counsellors Ruth might work with in Chapter 1, to illustrate this kind of influence. While it can be comforting to take the serendipitous view that clients will always get the counsellors they need this is rather naive. Certainly it will happen on occasions but there will also be times when clients get the very counsellor they do not need and suffer the consequences. I think we do well to recognise that this is part of the shadow of the role of counselling: that the humanity of the counsellor which is necessary to the process will also exert influence upon that process. This influence is variable and to some extent unpredictable, although as I have earlier suggested, each of us may come to recognise something of the profile of our effect as we gain in experience.

There may be another assessment issue arising out of this influencing effect, for it may be that the suitability of the specific counsellor for a particular client needs to be questioned. This judgement can be difficult and needs to weigh not only who might be the best counsellor but also the cost to the client of transferring at the stage this is being considered. Nevertheless it is part of the equation and is better tackled than left to fester. It does not serve the client to dismiss these considerations with the banal assumption that it will always, by some magical means, work out for the best in the end. As Rowan so honestly puts it: 'The hard-earned lesson here is that I cannot assume competence with all and sundry. This was hard because I did think at first that my approach was so flexible and so potent

that it could benefit anyone at all; it was painful to discover otherwise'
(1992: 108)

Unbidden knowledge

In many instances there is an educational component to counselling, with
the client learning some new perspective, new cognitive framework or
taking on new beliefs and values. This may be vital in order to achieve the
client's goals. Consider the example of Clare who came to counselling
because she was suffering from anxiety in the form of sudden panic attacks.
It became clear that she was generally unaware of her emotional experience, tending to operate in a cognitive fashion. Her counsellor discussed
this with her and proposed a way of working towards relieving the panic
attacks that involved increasing Clare's emotional awareness. Although
she thought this a little strange it made some sense to Clare and she agreed
to 'have a go'.

During the following few months she met regularly with her counsellor
and embarked on a number of emotional awareness-raising strategies. She
started keeping a 'feelings diary' and discussing her emotional experience
each week in counselling. They also explored her breathing patterns and
Clare tried out deep, slow breathing that she then used during the onset of
panic attacks. Gradually the frequency and duration of attacks diminished
and Clare and her counsellor both felt satisfied with her progress. The
counselling was brought to a conclusion with the understanding that Clare
could return if she felt the need in the future.

This would appear to have been a successful piece of counselling and
from many vantage points indeed it was. Clare had changed as a consequence and was now less cognitively oriented, paying much greater
heed to her emotional experience. I would generally consider this to be a
productive outcome if I were counselling a client such as Clare, as I suspect
many other counsellors would also. It is perhaps somewhat surprising then
that a few months after ending the original counselling work she returned
in a state of considerable distress. Clare described how, since completing
counselling, she had gradually become disillusioned with her job in market-
ing and had started looking around for other opportunities. She had taken
a different job, rather less well paid, as a fund raiser for a small charity.
There she had fallen in love with one of her colleagues and had proceeded
to have a passionate affair that ended in a stormy and chaotic break
up. Meanwhile her own very stable marriage of fifteen years seemed to be
falling apart at great cost to herself, her husband and their children.

We could dismiss all this as unrelated to the counselling, justify it as an
important growth opportunity for all involved or conclude that this was all

going to happen anyway. Indeed there is a psychological argument for suggesting that given her escalating panic attacks Clare was heading for some sort of emotional eruption when she first arrived for counselling. However, from another perspective it could be seen that the emotional work done with Clare to relieve her panic attacks has had dramatic and unwelcome side effects that have caused Clare and her family considerable anguish. What is known in this particular case is that although Clare did agree to engage with the goal of increasing her emotional awareness neither Clare nor her counsellor foresaw the consequences. I do not presume to say that she should not have received counselling or that the counselling should have taken a different form. However, I do believe that this is one example of an aspect of the counselling process that is paid insufficient heed. In my view Clare was encouraged to increase her emotional awareness with little regard paid to her inadequate resources for dealing with the results. In a sense she was plunged into the emotional turmoil most commonly associated with adolescence but without expecting this to occur. As a middle-aged adult with an established life this was very hard for her to manage. In fact she and her husband were able to hold their marriage together and gradually the storm subsided. But she had changed and it took considerable work for Clare and her husband to re-establish their relationship on a new basis that accommodated the changes she had made. In my view the shadow side of this particular tale lies not in what occurred but that a legitimate therapeutic strategy could have such difficult, and unforeseen, secondary consequences.

When talking doesn't help: the hothouse that desiccates

There are undoubtedly clients who come to counselling and are palpably relieved having put into words what they have previously been holding inside. This is one of the functions of the role: to provide a safe and private space where the unspoken can be said, and heard, without undue judgement or reaction. But there are other clients who may indicate that they have had intensely painful past experiences without disclosing much, if any, detail of the actual events. Yet there is an implicit assumption within therapeutic work that it is valuable to talk about events that are troubling. In a thought-provoking article Kempler (1987) raises questions about the universal usefulness of articulating innermost feelings or secret experiences. It is clearly a valuable process for some but he is raising the possibility that for others it can be counterproductive.

In my own practice I have noticed that a small number of clients have a marked reluctance to discuss the very experiences that are sources of pain to them. I am not referring to the inevitable reluctance that most feel prior to talking about painful events. That is an entirely understandable hesitation before moving into raw feelings, but a hesitation that the client can be gently encouraged to overcome. The reluctance of a few is of a different order, a strong resistance that is not simply moved through but a palpable barrier to disclosure. Sometimes this generates quite intense feelings of frustration in me that have every appearance of a countertransference response to the client's desire to withhold their experience from me. In dynamic terms this seems an entirely legitimate experiment by the client, perhaps redressing previous occasions when they felt exposed, required to do something against their wishes or violated in some other way. I have come to respect the potential therapeutic value in this particular process of withholding and now believe that for some this may be the primary therapeutic task. It is conceivable that in so doing they reclaim the personal power that was effectively stolen from them during the original experiences.

One way that I have of understanding this process is that it reflects the client's need to incubate their experience, holding it within themselves until the right moment to allow it to be born. The analogy of the butterfly and the chrysalis seems apt: if the butterfly tries to rush the process of emerging, or we try to hurry the pace in our desire to be helpful, then disaster will result. Kempler (1987) talks of ideas that, if shared prematurely, lose their strength in some way. It is very probable that this is true on occasions of the insight that can emerge during therapeutic work.

The potential element of role shadow in this regard results from the assumption underlying counselling generally that it 'helps to talk'. This can result in clients feeling that they should disclose and therefore override their instinctive reluctance. This becomes even more potent if it is combined with a counsellor who believes in the universal efficacy of disclosure and so exerts a degree of pressure on the client to do so. The result may be an unhelpful process that adds to the sense of shame and exposure of the client without any significant level of healing taking place. This is a speculative possibility as I have no firm evidence that this does indeed take place and measuring such an effect is likely to be very problematic. However, I have had a small number of clients who have made it clear that they are withholding significant information from me. I have also had a few clients who have recounted experiences in a manner that has left me uncomfortable. When this has happened I have felt that they have been exposing something of themselves to me in a manner that has felt unwholesome.

The stigma of counselling

Unfortunately there are instances in which attendance for counselling subsequently comes to light in a way which works against the best interests of the client. There are a number of ways in which this can happen and as counselling becomes increasingly accepted within organisational contexts the potential for such situations probably becomes greater. The process of stigmatisation and how it relates to identity and social standing has been explored in detail by Goffman (1963). It can occur if, for example, attending counselling is routinely recorded onto a person's employment or medical record. Such recording is generally done in all innocence and for understandable practical reasons. However, it is then not possible to control the future ways this information may be used. I have heard of instances where the person's use of counselling has been included in a reference for employment because the referee genuinely believed that the potential employer had a right to have this information.

At the heart of such difficulties lies the range of meanings that can be ascribed to having been a client. As counsellors we are probably all sympathetic and would tend to read this information as a sign of maturity or awareness. Certainly as someone who is sometimes in the situation of employing counsellors a candidate's experience as a client is something that I consider to be very much in their favour. This may be true for other helping professions, although there is currently an increasing concern within nursing in the UK about use of counselling. This is a direct consequence of the identification of 'excessive use of counselling' (Clothier 1994: 84) as an indicator of personality disorder that was the diagnosis of Beverley Allitt, the enrolled nurse who was convicted for the murder of four children in her care. As a result of the enquiry into this tragedy nurses' use of counselling has become a cause for concern within the Health Service.

In general going for counselling is often taken as a sign of weakness, of vulnerability or fragility, perhaps as a sign of some emotional or psychological instability. Actually none of these general meanings being attributed to attending counselling bear any other than purely coincidental relation to what it means for a particular individual. It is to be hoped that the person will be asked about having been a client so that assumptions about what it means can be tested. Nevertheless there will inevitably be occasional instances where simply the fact of having been a client will be detrimental to the individual in some way and we would be naive to believe otherwise. In part the implications of this are educational, for as counselling becomes increasingly recognised as a normal resource that 'ordinary' people can use at times of particular stress or distress so the stigma will, presumably, reduce. At present counselling undoubtedly still carries associations for some people of weakness or mental instability. As counsellors I believe that we have some responsibility to try to minimise the likelihood that our clients will be stigmatised in this manner. We cannot ensure this, but we can treat the possibility with the degree of seriousness it warrants.

THE CLIENT'S PERSONAL SHADOW

The single summative conclusion that may be drawn is that counselling can be damaging to clients. However, it is not my wish to suggest that clients are simply passive and innocent victims of the vicissitudes of the counselling process. A proportion of the clients I see bring the need to know more of their shadow into our relationship. Usually this is done unconsciously and my task then is to find ways to enable the client to face this seemingly undesirable aspect of themselves, presuming that they are willing to do so, at a pace that they can tolerate. The kinds of shadow material a client may bring with them are as broad and varied as it is possible for personal shadow to be. There are particular aspects of personal shadow, however, that tend to resonate with being in the role of client. I want to consider three examples of this type of client shadow material:

- the tendency to want to remain a victim;
- seeking permission to 'act out';
- the desire for revenge.

I also want to consider some shadow possibilities in the specific situation when the client is also a counsellor.

Perpetuating victimhood

Far from encouraging the idea of client as victim I want to propose that the client who comes to counselling wanting to perpetuate their own sense of victimhood is in the thrall of their shadow. This stems from their personal shadow to the extent that it is an unconsciously driven desire, or need. There are some who present for counselling because they know that they are stuck in a sense of being a victim from events long gone and they want to find a way to break this pattern: to find a way to feel and act with responsibility for their own life. Such clients do not have their victimhood in their shadow, far from it.

To continue to be a victim is to be in a fixed psychological state (Shohet 1998), to think, feel and act on the basis that life will always be difficult and damaging and that we are powerless to do anything to change this. It is not possible to feel and act with responsibility while 'we assume that we are a poor wounded child and a victim of our parents, set to become a victim of society in our adult life' (Hall 1993: 147). With such a client our task as counsellor is a delicate one as we have to pick our way between the need for their powerful feelings to be validated and the need to encourage a more robust claiming of their current adult choices. In my experience it can sometimes take a great deal of care and patience to dislodge such a client from their belief in their own victimhood that may be one of the defining characteristics of their self-description. They may try to pull us into a collusive alliance and if we rush the task their level of fear may be such that they flee, dismissing us as yet one more powerful and persecutory person who did not understand their plight. They may do this anyway regardless of how delicately we tread as this provides further evidence for the victim view of the world: if even a counsellor doesn't understand me then the world really is against me.

Seeking permission to 'act out'

I sometimes find myself in a quandary with a client. I want to offer a level of acceptance that does not impose conditions as I believe that this can have a significant healing effect, but from time to time I am faced with someone who appears to want to act in a way that seems to be damaging to themselves or someone else. This can be particularly difficult to resolve when the client is doing something that sounds harmful to a vulnerable person. There has been much debate about this in the area of child protection: should we report and probably break up our therapeutic relationship in the process or should we undertake the therapeutic work that might lead to the behaviour stopping without intrusive investigations that can do more harm than good for the child? Jenkins (1997) has summarised the situation well, considering the dilemmas within a legal context. But what of the client who admits to beating an elderly relative, or depriving them of necessities in a cruel way? This old person is arguably as vulnerable as a child. Furthermore, an adult in a relationship who is being mistreated but for some reason feels unable to leave may be equally vulnerable in practice, if not appearing to be so in principle. In each of these instances the client's shadow may be in evidence in their perpetrating the harm or in their willingness to be the passive bystander while someone else is causing pain.

I do not have a simple answer, if I did it would not be a true dilemma. Rather we have to weigh up the various factors in each individual case and make what we genuinely believe to be the best decision under the circumstances. We may be relieved of some of this burden by working in positions where we are bound by nondiscretionary reporting policies relating to child protection and sometime vulnerable adults also. Such policies offer guidelines although the practitioner remains responsible for deciding how to proceed with a specific client. For me one of the questions I ask myself is: Do I believe that this client has a genuine desire to stop what is happening? My own answer to this does not necessarily determine what I do but certainly has a considerable influence. I have no wish to be drawn into colluding with a client who seems to want to take my acceptance of them as a person as equating with tacit permission to allow what is happening to continue.

Seeking revenge

From time to time a client arrives who seems intent on taking revenge upon the counsellor for some past perceived injustice. Jacobs suggests that 'revenge and retaliation . . . are an attempt to restore the fragile balance' (1996: 17), referring to the balance of superiority and inferiority in human relationships. It can be therapeutic for a client to enact revenge upon their counsellor, but only if the client is able to recognise what he or she is doing and learn from this. I am thinking of Ben who from the outset made comments that undermined and belittled the counsellor he was seeing. Ben was challenged, repeatedly, and the counsellor felt that they were making significant progress. Then as one session was ending and they moved towards the door Ben stepped across and took the counsellor in his arms in what was supposedly a grateful hug. The counsellor was frozen at the time and then had a mounting sense of fury for what she experienced as a physical violation. It was very hard for Ben to accept how the counsellor had experienced what he had done. Eventually he was able to link what had occurred to the purportedly affectionate acts that had been inflicted upon him as a child by various members of his family. It appeared that Ben needed his counsellor to live through an example of his own early experience in order to help him face the pain of this for himself.

Ben provides an example of a client who presents for counselling unconsciously wanting to break their pattern of revenge, to find a way out of the trap they have created for themselves. Shohet describes reaching this point in a conscious way when he says: 'I have now read enough remarkable stories of forgiveness, and had enough experiences of the destructiveness and seductiveness of vengeful fantasies, to want to break my personal addiction to vengeful thoughts' (1996: 4). As counsellors we need, for our own protection, to be watchful of clients such as Ben who may enact their vengeful fantasies upon us, presumably without realising that they are doing so. While this may ultimately be therapeutic for them the cost to us may be quite high, sometimes higher than it is wise to pay. I am thinking of another client who came to counselling apparently to work through his feelings about the recent break up of his marriage. After each session the counsellor came away feeling battered and bruised without understanding why. The client ran up a bill for a few sessions and then simply didn't turn up one week. In reply to a letter from the counsellor asking him to pay the bill and suggesting a final session the client wrote that if it hadn't been for his wife being encouraged by her counsellor she would never have left him. He didn't pay his outstanding bill! This is an example of another sort of revenge where there seems little if any intention to work through the pain of what has occurred. The client simply took revenge upon the counsellor and then walked away, presumably believing that some balance had been restored, although in this case the balance is not in the context of a real relationship but remains in the fantasy of the client.

When the client is also a counsellor

There is a particular situation created when the client is also a practitioner as their personal shadow is quite likely to resonate with the role shadow. There are some relatively predictable elements to this of which both participants are likely to have some awareness. These include the potential for competition and rivalry between counsellor and client, pressure on the client to perform well in that role, attempts by the client to act as their own therapist and the counsellor feeling under constant scrutiny as the client assesses (or we perceive the client to be assessing) every intervention we make. Any one of these may interfere with useful therapeutic work, distracting from the central agenda of the client. However, it is also the case that the presence of these factors may result in an improved quality of therapeutic work, adding an edge to our performance.

What are perhaps more subtle and therefore more likely to remain unconscious are the dangers of distortion that also exist. When counsellor and client are both immersed in therapeutic thinking this can result in a lack of the healthy level of scepticism sometimes needed to temper the psychological perspective. If this occurs, then the interaction becomes ungrounded and may get lost in the emotional and psychological aspects of the client's experience. One example of this sort of danger is that of the client becoming very focused upon their own inner processes without due regard for the impact of this upon their personal life or career. This may well happen on occasions but if not gently challenged then it can have a detrimental effect upon the client's life. If we get caught up in the client's therapeutic process we may enter with them into a somewhat mesmerised state, neither of us noticing what is going on beyond the boundaries of the counselling session.

As counsellors we cannot ensure that coming to counselling is a constructive and positive experience for our clients. There will be occasions when this is not so. We can, however, be alert to the possibility that counselling is a negative experience and do everything within our power to minimise the likelihood of this happening. Similarly we cannot render ourselves impervious to clients' unconscious hostility or ensure that they recognise and move towards incorporating their shadow. We can be aware that they do have a shadow, just as we do, and endeavour to act in ways that take account of this and remain respectful of our clients and ourselves.

9   The shadow of the profession

In this final chapter I am shifting the focus away from the individual figures who are the principal subjects in the foreground of the counselling picture: the counsellor and the client. Instead I am turning attention to the background: the context or collective within which counselling occurs. This context will have its own 'collective shadow' (Jung 1970: 572) or 'cultural shadow' as it is sometimes known.[1] As with the shadow of individuals this collective shadow is unconscious, although a few members may be aware of aspects of what it contains. As collective shadow develops in parallel with the collective 'ego' or identity it will have its roots within the history of that collective, a history that may be long forgotten. The potency of the collective shadow will correspond to the strength of the collective ego or 'group ego' (Foulkes and Anthony 1984). This in turn is related to the degree to which individuals define themselves in terms of membership of the particular collective.

THE NATURE OF COLLECTIVE SHADOW

A collective may be any grouping of people: a whole nation, race, religion, corporation, educational community or a small clique. A topical example is provided by the celibate priesthood of the Roman Catholic Church: a grouping who avow to abstain from sexual activity. The shadow side of this particular collective is being painfully exposed as a number of instances of abusive sexual behaviour by a few of its members are being brought to public attention. There are also examples of groups committed to stopping violence being perpetrated upon the vulnerable who are themselves violent in their protests. This can be seen when animal rights activists threaten lives and damage property and anti-abortion demonstrators assault, and on occasions kill, medical personnel.

The essential process of collective shadow formation corresponds to that which occurs in the personal shadow. As the collective takes on an identity, or ego, so a shadow forms and takes shape. When the collective determines, as part of its identity, to emphasise a particular characteristic, the opposing aspect may be driven into unconsciousness. This is not a predetermined or necessary process of splitting, but it often occurs. Thus a group committed to pacifism is not necessarily doomed to exhibit violence, this will depend upon a range of factors. Perhaps the most critical is that if key individuals are psychologically disposed to deny and then project onto others their own violence then this will almost inevitably become part of that group's shadow. In contrast a pacifist group within which individuals are able to acknowledge their own aggressive instincts is much more likely to be successful in its peaceful endeavours. It is important to recognise that it is not the choice to manifest a particular characteristic or belief that results in shadow formation but rather the refusal to accept that at the same time we have the capacity for its opposite.

A collective will often contain a significant number of members who happily embrace the avowed position. Among those committed to protect the rights of animals there will be many for whom it is important to live in a manner that is respectful towards the rights of others, both animal and human. However, such a group will also have an appeal to some who want to deny their own aggressive and oppressive instincts, or justify their wish to be violent in the name of the cause. Similarly many Roman Catholic priests are devout and committed celibates who are willing to tolerate their sexual frustrations and indeed may find spiritual nourishment through living this commitment. However, this way of life will also attract some who are seduced by the power of the role and will abuse that power to satisfy their own poorly understood sexual desires, probably rationalising their behaviour as being loving or healing. Given this it is important not to condemn a whole group but rather to recognise that any collective that seeks to express a particular attribute of human behaviour that it considers desirable, be it peacefulness, generosity, celibacy, or equality, is likely on occasions to include individuals who manifest the opposing characteristic of violence, greed, sexual profligacy or dominance.

Running through these assertions is the theme of balance: that any characteristic has its counterbalancing opposite as a secondary function.[2] As with the personal shadow, there are a few examples where the attributes manifested by the collective shadow are not simply a weaker secondary function related to the manifestations of the collective ego but rather represents a positive destructive force. There are sufficient examples just in this century of groups that have been overtaken by their shadow to confirm that this can occur. Some have turned their shadow upon others: the excesses of Nazism and Stalinism stand out in this category. Others turn it upon themselves as witnessed in the events of Jonestown or Waco.[3] These collectives can be thought of as having been possessed by a particular aspect of the shadow archetype.

As counsellors we do not exist in isolation but rather we too have a context, both personal and professional. We each do well to explore how the collectives to which we belong personally may contribute to our shadow. My own cultural heritage is rooted within my upbringing as a white middle-class English man. Consequently I have to be aware that despite my best efforts there remain vestiges of xenophobic and racist beliefs within my unconscious. Many of my ancestors (and I fear some of my contemporaries) believed in their racial and cultural supremacy and on this basis justified slavery and domination of others. However much I abhor these dreadful practices and consciously refute the underlying beliefs I would be foolish to imagine that I can fully expunge these same beliefs from my own psyche. To believe that I can is likely to lead to the kind of unintentional racism that Ridley (1995) describes.

I need also to be watchful of my inherent middle-class values, for instance the spurious belief that all have the necessary resources and opportunities to create satisfying and fulfilling lives for themselves. These same values pervade parts of the world of counselling, which is some-times guilty of ignoring the impact of the enormous social injustices that dominate the lives of many. As a man I need to be aware of the unsolicited advantages my gender affords me while not submerging my masculinity in an attempt to purge myself of the guilt I sometimes feel in the face of these privileges. Alongside these I have also to contend with a propensity for depressive guilt, judgementalism and a deep longing to merge with an almighty being that rest in my psyche as a consequence of an upbringing within the Roman Catholic Church. At different times one or more of these elements of my personal heritage will be active within my shadow, influencing my thoughts, feelings and actions. The same is true for each of us, we never fully erase our heritage from our shadow and delude ourselves if we believe this to be achievable.

As counsellors we belong to the wider counselling collective in addition to the collectives that we are part of personally. We are all influenced by the shadow side of the counselling collective, whether or not we are active participants within that world. This influence is continuous, occurring at both a conscious and unconscious level and moving between the two. An example of this is the process whereby developments in therapeutic thinking move from being the radical idea of one or more individuals to become subsumed within the assumptions and beliefs of the general counselling population. In his book published in the 1980s Casement

(1985) introduced[4] the term 'internal supervisor' to describe a particular form of active self-reflection. This phrase is now in regular use in training courses, other publications and general discussion within the profession. When I was involved in interviewing for a course in counselling supervision (Page and Wosket 1994) it was one of the phrases that, quite understandably, many interviewees used in an effort to communicate to us their knowledge of the subject. It remains a matter of speculation as to how many of those who use the term in these various forums understand it in the manner in which it was offered by Casement, for often as ideas spread so they are modified and diluted. Nevertheless it has become absorbed within the therapeutic vocabulary, having spread from that initial publication through to general usage. It is not strictly unconscious, but many who use the term will be quite unaware of its roots in Casement's work.

Similarly there have been considerable developments over the last decade in relation to an understanding of childhood trauma and abuse (Miller 1987). This has played a significant part in the evolution of therapeutic thinking, with the increased use of models involving the inner child within the adult survivor (another relatively new term, I suspect). The energy fuelling the recent backlash of the so-called 'false memory syndrome' lobby (Enns 1996; Pope 1996) is testimony to the raw state of the nerve this particular debate has touched. These are simple examples of the process of development that takes place continually within the counselling and therapeutic field. We will variously be aware of some elements of this process and unaware of others. Many of these influences merge into the background, absorbed into the collective identity of counselling and passed on to future practitioners in the assumptions and assertions that are made. Some will sink sufficiently to enter into the collective counselling shadow where they can be but dimly perceived and yet exert an influence.

One way in which we take in elements of the collective shadow is through the particular counselling organisations or settings in which we practice. To illustrate this I would like to consider three examples of formative experiences in my own development as a counsellor. The first was while studying at university in the 1970s being part of a student-run drop-in facility for fellow students. This was an excellent amateur service that offered much both to its users and to those students acting as volunteer 'listeners'. However, with hindsight I recognise that it had a component to its shadow side which is often found in voluntary schemes: there was an underpinning assumption that the service had to be there for everyone. This resulted on occasions in inexperienced volunteers being put upon by demanding users, or overwhelmed by trying to cope with acutely distressed or disturbed people, sometimes putting at risk the personal safety of all concerned. The desire to provide a service for students in need was not matched by an equal concern for the well-being of those, from the same student body, who were providing the service.

Later I worked in residential therapeutic communities for people with a range of mental health difficulties, staffed predominantly by bright and idealistic young graduates. Again I remain respectful of the work we did and the opportunities provided both for the residents living in those communities and for the staff working in them. However, there were a range of shadow elements in these communities, one example being an influential anti-psychiatry tendency. On some occasions this led to people being discouraged from seeking much needed psychiatric support and a pervasive sense that taking prescribed medication was somehow 'failing'. Given that a considerable proportion of these residents were likely (when judging pragmatically rather than idealistically) to require long-term psychiatric intervention this was most unfortunate. But it followed almost inevitably from the deeply held humanistic views that became enmeshed with the unresolved rebelliousness (Heron 1990) with which many of the workers were still contending. This ideology was not always tempered by the willingness or capacity to discern who, at any given time, was able to fully take responsibility for themselves and who was not.

My third example comes from an intensive humanistic-oriented group in which I participated. While this was one of the most transforming experiences of my adult life it too had a shadow side, much of which I struggled to recognise at the time. The particular aspect I recall was the belief that all feelings needed to be expressed through catharsis. At times this resulted in levels of pressure on individuals to 'go for it' which I look back on now and see as sometimes unhelpful and on occasions abusive. Some members were reluctantly coerced into doing personal therapeutic work and others were encouraged to address, through catharsis, feelings that did not break down into simple emotional components and therefore were not readily accessible to cathartic release (Heron 1992). Being quite emotionally repressed I was particularly susceptible to this belief as it dovetailed with my own real need to be more emotionally expressive. As a result of my experiences in this group I had to struggle as a counsellor with this idea of catharsis as panacea, and for a while this did impair my practice.

These three examples highlight particular tendencies that may have become part of the impact of collective shadow upon those, like myself, involved in those particular groupings. Each of them, the lack of self-protective boundaries, the anti-psychiatry ideology and the overemphasis on the value of cathartic expression, are potentially quite insidious influences. We can all critically examine our own experiences in those parts of the counselling collective with which we have been particularly involved and to assist in this task there are a number of perspectives that can be taken up. I want to go on to outline three such viewpoints and offer examples of their application.

The principle of opposites

Guggenbühl-Craig describes the collective shadow as 'the dark other side of the collective ideal' (1971:112). Applying this formulation to any counselling community implies that a part of the collective shadow is to be found on the 'dark other side' of the ideals of that collective. I felt that I observed an example of this principle of opposites at work in a counsellor training institute founded on humanistic principles that place particular emphasis upon equity and minimising imbalances of power within therapeutic relationships (Rowan 1988). This particular training organisation required all trainees to undertake a substantial amount of personal therapy during their training. However, the choice of therapist was very restricted, the options effectively being one of the core trainers or associates. When challenged by trainees this was denied but a number of attempts to have other therapists accepted as suitable alternatives were all unsuccessful, even though some of those offered were of considerable experience and standing as practitioners. The paradox is clear: an organisation seemingly committed to equality is exercising power in a cavalier way and seemingly oblivious to the inherent contradiction in its actions. This lack of awareness of the inconsistency between beliefs and particular actions is typical when the collective shadow is present. Responses to challenges did nothing to convince the challengers, leaving them feeling unheard and fobbed off.

Imposed ideology

Another way in which an ideal becomes part of the shadow of a counselling collective is when it is formed into an ideology that is then imposed in an indiscriminate manner. When this occurs the autonomy of clients is being undermined as they are pressured to move in a particular direction. At worst this becomes a route into cultist behaviour, although there are considerably milder examples where this same process appears to be in operation.

One such was an organisation committed to working with women from a particular ethnic group. The client group included many young women who were finding themselves under considerable pressure to accept the marriage partners their parents had chosen for them. While the organisation was very successful in helping a considerable number of these young women it essentially did so by enabling them to leave their family and community, making a new life elsewhere. For many this was probably the only realistic way forward, however, some went to the organisation hoping for support to remain within their family. In counselling, these clients found themselves under considerable pressure to leave their family and offered little support for their preferred path. It took persistent urging from a number of quarters before this organisation reviewed its approach and started to offer mediation and educational sessions for the young women and their families alongside individual counselling. Until it did this it was essentially imposing an ideology: that the only way forward was to leave family and community. Once it offered a range of options it was able to encourage the clients to make their own choice and offer them resources to support this decision.

This example was chosen because it is readily apparent that what was taking place was undermining of therapeutic usefulness. There are other occasions when it is harder to distinguish between what is therapeutically appropriate and an imposed ideology. The litmus test that can be applied is that of conditionality, when acceptance of the client is conditional upon their choosing certain options and rejecting others then it is likely that the client is having an ideology imposed upon them.

The critical comparative

Identity is formulated by a recognition of one's own unique characteristics and also by comparison of these characteristics with those that others display. This is true not only for individuals but also for groups and so will be one way in which the identity of the counselling collective has been formulated. The desire to create identity through comparison is reminiscent of the struggles that go on for individuals during the period of adolescence. Young people in this developmental stage (Erikson 1977) will often be involved in defining identifying characteristics for themselves, both as individuals and in groups. This can be done by formulating group identity that contrasts sharply with other groups, typically with the parent generation but also with other groups within their own age group.

There is much opportunity for shadow generation in this process as any uncertainties or insecurities about the group's identity can readily be channelled into attacks upon the contrasting groups. On a global scale this mechanism can be seen at work in racism, xenophobia and hostility to perceived enemies. Indeed few international news broadcasts, however brief, will not include reports on fighting between rival factions in one part of the world or another. To anyone not involved in a particular conflict the apparent reasons for inflicting great suffering and death can seem remarkably absurd and utterly disproportionate: some small piece of disputed territory, differences in belief, grudges for grievances perpetrated by the long dead ancestors of one group against those of another and so on. While not wishing to oversimplify such dreadful human situations the prevalence of intractable conflict in the collective history of our species does seem to be an indicator of the depth to which the need to belong to a particular group can reach into the human psyche. Soth (1992) offers an interesting exploration of these processes in the context of the 1991 Gulf War. He describes the parallels in a group he ran to examine what could be learnt from this war and the actual conflict itself and offers his conviction 'that if we were to fully recognise just how all-pervasively personal the political is, it would blow our minds' (ibid.: 36).

As counsellors we are not involved in any bloody struggle but nevertheless are sometimes prey to quite significant rivalries with other professional groups. This may be with psychiatrists, psychologists, psychoanalysts, psychotherapists, nurses, alternative health practitioners or general physicians. It may be between the psychoanalytically oriented and the humanistic, or either of these and the cognitive- or behavioural-oriented practitioners. There are significant distinguishing features between all these different groups and identifying these differences can be useful. However, I want to look specifically at the shadow side, where rational comparison falls away into critical attack as a defence against our own insecurities.

Take as an example the profession of clinical psychology. As counsellors we might sneer a little and dismiss them as only being concerned to change behaviour, with little regard to the long-term consequences for the client. But how often would we wish to find a way to achieve this very result: to help the anorexic client eat, the anxious client to relax, the addict to kick the habit. Indeed some counsellors do employ techniques that have been developed in the more cognitive and behavioural fields. Nevertheless I suspect that within some areas of the collective shadow there remains a somewhat superior sense that such 'tricks' are not really what counselling is about. I make this assertion somewhat ruefully from my own recent experience when a clinical psychologist joined the team I manage on a sessional basis some months ago. Surprised at the range of feelings I found myself experiencing – suspicion, envy, anxiety and shame for my own perceived inadequacies with clients I referred to her – I have now come not only to respect her work and be glad to have this resource for clients I work with but also to recognise how much more alike than different our two therapeutic approaches actually are. I thought that I knew all this before from my previous constructive dealings with a number of clinical psychologists over the years. But that was always at arm's length and we each maintained our own territorial boundaries. Inviting someone from that profession within my work boundaries touched another level of my vulnerability and activated critically defensive responses that I had not previously known.

Identifying the collective shadow

Each of these three perspectives, the principle of opposites, imposed ideology and the critical comparative offer ways of identifying the involvement of collective shadow. The presence of repetition in different places and at varying times is also a very good indicator that a particular action has its primary roots within the collective shadow. It is difficult to conclude in any one instance the different ingredients of collective and personal shadow that have produced the cocktail out of which the act has emerged. However, when a type of behaviour is repeated by a number of different individuals in different places and at different times then it is reasonable to presume a collective component at work. Repeating themes, issues that keep emerging however many attempts are made at resolution, or boundaries that regularly spring a leak are all indicators that the collective shadow may be at work.

THE COMMUNITY PERSPECTIVE

The next perspective from which I shall consider the potential consequences of the shadow of the role of counselling is that of the community within which it takes place. My purpose is to reflect upon the possibility that counselling not only brings benefits to society but also may, in some ways, be detrimental. It is my view that as counsellors we do have a responsibility to be open and alert to such a potentiality, as this renders us more able to act should social costs of our counselling activities start to become visible.

Dissipating community action

Counselling does by its nature focus at an individual level, and its theoretical constructs are primarily based around the psychology of the individual person (Dryden 1990). There are also models that are concerned with working with couples (Hooper and Dryden 1991), families (Treacher and Reimers 1994) or groups (Corey 1995) but they each remain rooted in a psychological perspective. The task of the counsellor is to try, through an authentic relationship, to enable individuals in the client role to move through and beyond current difficulties by finding and mobilising their own resources. As has already been emphasised it is not the role of a counsellor to promote a particular sociological or political position and indeed to do so is an improper use of the power invested in the role. Thus the counselling focus tends to be primarily upon the emotional and psychological needs of the client, the aim being to promote development in some form. This is not intrinsically damaging but there may be a shadow side to it when considering a particular situation from the viewpoint of the wider community.

What of the town where the major employer in the area is to close? While it may well be of benefit to many of the individuals affected by this experience if a team of redundancy counsellors are sent into the town, this does nothing to resolve the main issue from the perspective of the community. For the central issue is not that individual employees have been made redundant, even though for those people this will probably have been a distressing experience. The central issue for the community is that its local economy has been fundamentally damaged and many of those same redundant employees will not have jobs unless steps are taken to increase local employment.

The danger then is that the team of counsellors are seen as a solution to the problem when they are merely a means of transitory support for some individuals who have been badly affected. The counselling is humane and decent but secondary to the deeper needs of developing local employment and reconstructing a healthy thriving community. It is to be hoped that this is well recognised and understood and the counsellors are just one of a number of forms of support and input. Should the counselling intervention be seen as a resolution then it can be argued that it has been a disservice to the local community.

To put this in more symbolic language it is possible for counselling to be expected to fulfil the role of great mother archetype[5] for society. When someone is bruised and bleeding they are sent along to be metaphorically held and comforted and when necessary, patched up with sticking plaster. But attention must be paid to the causes of the bruising and bleeding, with action taken when possible to deal with these causes before other individuals get hurt. The social danger is that there is a general sigh of relief when 'mother' appears so that the energy and commitment to solving the more fundamental social and political problems may be dissipated.

As counsellors we may get unwittingly drawn into such situations without any real insight into the dubious benefits resulting from our services being proffered. We may not have an opportunity to see the work we are doing in a broader context, although arguably this is a responsibility we all carry. Even if there is the possibility to see the counselling input within the wider picture some counsellors, operating from individual and psychological perspectives, may not have the awareness to draw the appropriate conclusions. Training as a counsellor often gives a quite restricted psychologically based view of the nature of human suffering and difficulties. Whitmore (quoted in Horton *et al.* 1995) does speak encouragingly of signs of change with increasing focus in counsellor training on multiculture, gender, class, race and social issues. This is very much needed if we are to comprehend the setting within which counselling is taking place. Such training coupled with a system-oriented understanding can develop what Handy has described as 'the helicopter factor' (1985): the ability to rise above the immediate and view the overall landscape.

Another of the possible unhelpful consequences of counselling is that those determined to change situations may find their passion, their level of energy to take action, dissipates as they talk through their experiences. There is the possibility that through expressing feelings in the consulting room there remains less incentive to act decisively in the offending situation. This is not determinedly so, through counselling some may feel more able to act, more focused and clear about the direction they want to take. However, the possibility remains that counselling will act to ameliorate passions that otherwise might be put to good effect. I recall a client referred to me by her employer because she was off sick from work as a result of stress. We did some successful counselling work together in that she was able to move on, leave her job and find new ways forward for herself. But what of her employment situation which was clearly the cause of many of her difficulties? When she arrived she was angry and wanted to seek ways to change the situation at her place of work. This would be a passionate response, using her anger to endeavour to correct what she perceived to be wrong, to bring about change. But she left that behind as we looked to her future, her anger subsided to be replaced with interest and excitement about the possibilities that lay before her.

I view this as an example of the kind of energy that may be dissipated through the emotional expression encouraged in counselling. I doubt that it is possible to determine a causal relationship but there is a case for suggesting that the expression of passionate feelings in the consulting room deprives society of that energy that might otherwise be put to useful social purpose. Hillman puts this succinctly when, talking particularly about therapy that encourages a focus on childhood experience, he says: "'All I can do is go into myself, work on my growth, my development, find good parenting, support groups." This is a disaster for our political world, for our democracy. Democracy depends on intensely active citizens, not children' (Hillman and Ventura 1992: 6).

Counselling and prevention

It is essential to recognise the uncomfortable truth that 'one-to-one treatment, medical or psychological, does not, and cannot, affect incidence' (Albee, 1994: 2). The implications for counsellors are that our work with clients does nothing to reduce the level of damage being inflicted upon other individuals. There is a small caveat in that a successful client who has been mistreated may not go on to inflict the same mistreatment upon the next generation, which they might have done without counselling. However, this level of prevention is not statistically significant in the context of the overall prevalence of psychological difficulties. Studies carried out on general population groups maintain that between 37 and 55 per cent have a significant level of psychological difficulty (Opler 1969). Clearly only a very small proportion of these people will ever access counselling or any other type of formal therapeutic assistance.

Considering these levels of psychological and emotional difficulties there is an argument for suggesting that counselling depletes resources that might have greater effect if used in other ways. This parallels the debates that go on in relation to medicine: a great many people might be prevented from contracting heart disease if the resources which go into one heart transplant operation were used instead to fund education programmes in healthy diet and physical fitness. Similarly it can be argued that more would be achieved if the salary for a counsellor were used to pay for a health promotion educator to provide, for example, classes in parenting skills and stress management. This is an element of health promotion, providing people with resources that, it is hoped, will enable them to foster their own well-being (Tudor 1996). It is hard to square up one single equation that contains remedial, preventative and promotional factors. It is also naive to believe that resources are easily transferable between these different activities. However, as counsellors we need to face the possibility that our efforts may not be the best route to improving mental health or emotional well-being across the general population (MacDonald 1993).

In this context counselling is, at best, one element of a multilevel approach that provides remedial help to those in difficulty, preventative work with those identified as vulnerable and promotional activity that is both targeted to specific groups and applied across the general population. This would involve a range of disciplines of which counselling would be but one. However, many of us would need to make a considerable shift of paradigm in order to accommodate ourselves within such a schema. It would require counsellors seeing clearly beyond the confines of the consulting room, which is hard when so much work has gone into containing our focus in that setting. But if we do not do so it is possible that we will be at best uncooperative and at worst undermining of this more comprehensive strategy that is needed if there is to be any significant reduction in incidence.

Marginalising suffering

In a haunting tale Ursula Le Guin (1976) describes the need of a social group, in this case the population of a mythical town, to have those who carry the collective pain. The story describes how a child has to live in degradation in a dark cellar in order that the well-being of the rest of the population remains assured. This is a dramatic form of scapegoating[6] (Douglas 1995), the process where one person, or animal, is expected to carry away the sins of the whole community. It is somewhat far-fetched to draw the parallel between the whimpering child in the cellar and the clients who seek counselling. This would imply that every client is carrying distress on behalf of the community, which may be a realistic interpretation for some but not for the majority.

Clients may, however, be meeting social expectations by keeping their distress out of general view. The consulting room, then, becomes one haven for those who suffer, safe in the knowledge that their distress will be contained within that place. For the individuals themselves this may be a source of great relief, but it does have the effect of shutting the distress and pain out of the common sight. I am left wondering whether this may result in an increased inability and unwillingness within society to deal with manifestations of these difficult feelings. If this is the case it is the antithesis of what we might wish would result from the increased availability of counselling, for it is to be hoped that counselling will have a positive impact, with such effects as increasing the sense of compassion, the level of what Heron describes as 'emotional competence' (1990: 12) and the willingness to acknowledge and value affective experience. There are individuals who take up and act upon these values, and this may extend into groups or networks but it remains localised.[7] This is perhaps inevitable when considering that counselling is but one minor source of potential influence dwarfed by the political, economic and social changes that are constantly moulding and reshaping the social climate. However, should counselling add to an increased intolerance towards open emotional expression this would be a sad manifestation of its shadow.

THE COUNSELLING PROFESSION AND ITS SHADOW

The counselling movement in the United Kingdom has grown at a remarkable pace in the last twenty years, following behind a similar growth in the United States in the preceding decades (Gerstl 1969). This swift rate of expansion has been likened by Bond (1998) to the rapid development in the computer industry. The impact of the growth in the computer sector is easily visible, with many households now owning personal computers,[8] often complete with CD-Roms and modems. Similarly many office desks have their own stand-alone machines or network terminals with access to internet, e-mail and a vast array of software.

The impact of the growth of counselling is somewhat less clear, in part because it is cloaked in a shroud of confidentiality that generates an inevitable degree of mystery. The scale of counselling activity is considerable with Bond (1998) quoting a Department of Employment estimate that in 1993 over two and a half million people used counselling, including counselling skills, in their work. It is possible to find evidence of the growth in counselling, the 'tidal wave' that Jacobs (quoted in Horton *et al.* 1995) refers to, and its visibility to the general population in a number of ways beyond simply counting those who describe themselves as practitioners. The considerable array of volumes in the counselling section of bookshops and the number of counselling courses available do provide hints as to its new popularity but that is the specialist end of the counselling market. What is perhaps more telling is the increased frequency with which counselling is discussed in programmes on both television and radio. Also the pages of popular magazines and newspapers will often have articles on, or references to, counselling or therapy. In these various media there are those who are supportive of the important benefits of counselling and others who decry it as unhelpful or indulgent. This is an inevitable consequence of being part of the popular culture and the ensuing debates between detractors and defenders is one of the ways in which any newly recognised activity becomes absorbed into the collective consciousness. In the United Kingdom counselling would appear to have now established a place for itself within the national culture.

There are a number of challenges facing the counselling collective, or profession as it is fast becoming. One of these challenges is to recognise that aberrant behaviour by individuals may have its roots in the collective shadow and not merely be unfortunate isolated instances. In group terms collective shadow formation can lead to a process of denial identifiable through scapegoating, which I have already referred to earlier (see p. 145). If the desire in the majority to aspire to a particular ideal somehow shifts into the collective delusion that the ideal is being attained then denial is at work. Once this happens, once a significant proportion of a group believe themselves to be invulnerable to specific human frailties, then any who do manifest the particular attribute that is being denied are likely to be pilloried. In attacking those who make mistakes there is an unconscious wish to heap all the potential to act in this way onto those few who are unfortunate enough to do so. As such they become the scapegoats of the community and can then be sacrificed for what is believed to be the greater good. Jung (1959a: 469) warns of this difficulty in our current social context when he describes how the collective shadow figure 'gradually breaks up under the impact of civilisation, leaving traces in folklore that are difficult to recognise' with the consequence that 'the main part of him gets personalised and made an object of personal responsibility'.

I am not excusing individuals who act in a damaging manner towards a client, this must be dealt with appropriately by the profession in order to minimise the possibility of a recurrence. I support, and have some involvement in, the work of codifying ethical and sound practice and hearing complaints against counsellors, trainers and supervisors who may have gone outside these codes. However, this needs to be done in a spirit of humility, recognising that each of us might have acted similarly under certain circumstances. If it is done self-righteously, if the counsellor who has acted wrongly is unduly punished or vilified, then it is likely that some element of scapegoating is taking place. This in turn serves to fuel the collective shadow and in so doing makes it more likely that once the current scapegoat has been sacrificed this aspect of the shadow will find some other unfortunate individual through which to manifest itself.

Writing when chair of the BAC complaints committee Palmer-Barnes outlined common reasons for complaints. She cites 'poor understanding between client and counsellor about the nature of contract', trainees feeling that 'the goal posts have been moved during training' and 'counselling services need to be clear about what they can offer' (all quoted in Horton *et al.* 1995: 36). The emphasis therefore is on the need for greater clarity, which is also the reason for many of the revisions and subdivisions of codes of ethics and practice. While I welcome this trend I also think that it brings certain dangers with it. I know that I can be easily seduced by clarity, which was described by Don Juan as one of the enemies of people seeking knowledge and understanding (Castenada 1970). Indeed I suspect that it is my desire for clarity that attracts me to codes in the first place. Nevertheless I am of the view that clarity can assist in balancing power between counsellor and client, trainee and trainer, supervisee and supervisor. The clarity of 'contract' providing the container for the 'space' (Page and Wosket 1994) in which chaos and uncertainty can then occur. For the profession the parallel is to provide the clarity of boundaries within which uncertainty and dialogue can take place, the danger being that the boundaries, the professional structures, create a false sense of security rather than an environment within which difference and debate can be nurtured.

Similar tensions need to be held in the professional activity of accreditation and registration. Some are determined of the need for such procedures and there are certainly compelling arguments in terms of regulation, promoting client safety and improving quality of practice. There are also many warning shouts from those, such as Wasdell (1992), who consider this process to be driven more by fear and economics than any true attempt to increase the quality of practice. Somewhere between the potential extremes Frankland (1996) offers an attractively unassuming yet committed description of the middle ground from someone involved directly in a major counsellor accreditation scheme. When I applied for counsellor accreditation some years ago my conscious intention was pragmatic in that I saw it as another way of establishing my credentials as a practitioner. I was also seeking a way to respond to the insecurity that I felt, although I discovered that achieving accredited status did not diminish this insecurity to any appreciable degree. There is considerable insecurity and fear that gets focused on accreditation: fear of not being good enough, not being accepted, a paranoid fear of being 'found out' for some unspecified failing. Some respond to their fear as I did by applying to become accredited. In contrast it is also possible that some express their fear through criticising accreditation processes, as Wasdell puts it: 'Some of the rebellion against accreditation may be fear lurking in the shadows' (1992: 5).

There are many challenges facing the counselling collective in the various activities of professionalising that seem set to continue over the coming years. I think that one of the more difficult is to find a way to hold in our conscious view the shadow side of what we create. This should not stop us from moving forward, from being willing to respond to the developmental needs as they emerge. Indeed it should not stop us from enjoying this process. I certainly consider myself very lucky to have landed in a field of work that is in such a fascinating period of its development. Rather the shadow needs to be used as a reminder not to get too full of our own importance when admiring our own creations. We do well to remember that people have struggled and had difficulties or experienced tragic events throughout human history and those around or touched by the events have tended to naturally provide the necessary human support (Barton 1969). Indeed the relative, friend, neighbour or colleague are often still in the best position to offer what is needed, as they know the person, or people, involved. Also they are not restricted by the boundaries and structures within which we do, and must, operate as counsellors.

Notes

Introduction

1 Throughout the text I use the term 'counsellor' in its broadest sense to include those who would describe themselves as a therapist, psychotherapist, counselling psychologist, therapeutic counsellor or use a different term to define some other comparable therapeutic role.

2 Projection describes the process by which some undesirable aspect of ourselves is attributed to another person. Paranoid feelings are an example of projection in which we are afraid of someone else to whom we attribute some hostile intent. In a paranoid state the hostility is our own but in our fantasy is projected into another person, or object.

3 When material is quoted from the Collected Works of C. G. Jung the Arabic number in the brackets refers to the numbered paragraph from which the quote is taken. In all other quotes in the text the number that appears after the year of publication refers to the page number on which the text occurs.

4 I realise that my use of the term 'shadow' and its association of darkness and evil can be viewed as my using language that perpetuates racist associations. It is not my intention to cause offence and I hope that I do not. I have used this term because it has an important history within therapeutic language and it has a readily understood meaning. The primary purpose of this book is to encourage greater ownership and acknowledgement of those aspects of ourselves that we prefer to deny. When this occurs the need to project onto others our 'bad' selves should reduce. As this is one way of understanding the psychological component of racist thinking I believe it follows that the effect of this book should be to decrease rather than increase unintentional racism.

1 Counsellor: person, shadow and mask

1 Certain processes in the physical realm require an agent to act as an initiator and this agent can then be described as the activator (it is also a form of catalyst). An everyday example is that involving the mixing together of two substances to form a powerful glue. Often the components come in two separate containers: one substance is the glue and the other the activator. The glue does not work without the activator but the activator plays no part itself in the bonding, it simply enables the glue to perform its function.

2 Persona is the image of ourselves that we present to the world. The word derives from the Latin word for 'mask', as was used in classical theatre.

3 Winnicott (1965) offered the concept of true self, linking it to the capacity to be creative and spontaneous which he describes in terms of the capacity to play. The false self, or caretaker self, is rigid and defended, therefore unable to exhibit the characteristics of play. The latter is necessary for social development but is best balanced by the ability to move into the true self in an appropriate context.

4 Resonance in physics relates specifically to a phenomenon that can occur in oscillating systems. It describes what happens when one oscillating system induces oscillation in another system. This happens when both systems have the same, or very similar, frequency of oscillation (Marks 1967). For example, an elastic band vibrated will set off a visible vibration in a nearby band which is stretched to a similar degree of tension. This principle is used when tuning string instruments: if one string is tuned from a pure source such as a tuning fork all the other strings can then be tuned by fingering the tuned string to match the note wanted in the next string and so on.

3 Denying the shadow

1 The collective unconscious was thought by Jung to represent the 'repository of man's psychic heritage and possibilities' (Samuels *et al.* 1986: 32). I think of it as the collective human psychic field into which we tap at times. It is from this collective that we access archetypes.

2 In the Hindu tradition 'guru' is a general term whereas the 'Sad-Guru' is the true guru or teacher, being one who has reached the state of liberation or *moksha*. The archetype of guru would more accurately read the archetype of Sad-Guru for someone from within the Hindu tradition. It would also follow that anyone, including a counsellor, who tried to emulate the Sad-Guru without the accompanying wisdom and spiritual experience would come to grief.

3 'e-mail' is an abbreviation for electronic mail which describes sending and receiving messages between computers via the internet. There are currently a range of counselling and psychotherapy e-mail discussion forums, some general as well as ones intended for those working with specific client groups or working from particular orientations or disciplines.

4 Recognising the shadow

1 The name of this cat, N'Assarudin, was a cross between two other names. One was the name given to the wise-fool figure Mulla Nasrudin (Shah 1974), who features in many Sufi teaching stories. The other was Mohammed Azizuddin Azharuddin, who at the time was a much-acclaimed young member of the Indian Test cricket team. He created a record by scoring centuries in his first three Test matches and he went on to be their most successful captain in both Test matches and One Day Internationals. (For more information see the internet site: www.http://york.cricket.org:8000/link)

2 Racker (1968) distinguished between *concordant syntonic countertransference* in which the counsellor's response fits with the transferential content and *complementary syntonic countertransference* in which the counsellor's response is in opposition. For example, a client with a nurturing mother transference directed towards their counsellor might elicit a concordant nurturing response or a complementary stern or withholding response.

3 I am using the term 'projective identification' in this instance to describe a

process of affective communication whereby the client finds a means to communicate directly what they are feeling. The counsellor then feels something of what the client is feeling: a kind of emotional resonance. As Casement (1985) points out the term does get used in a range of different ways and this is but one of these.

4 The principle of 'half-life' is to be found in atomic physics where radioactive substances are described as having a half-life. This refers to the time period it takes for the substance to become half as radioactive as its initial level. For example, the naturally occurring element radium (Ra) has a half-life of 1,622 years (Marks 1967), so if a piece of radium has an initial level of radioactivity of 100 curies then after 1,622 years it will have a radioactivity of 50 curies, and after another 1,622 years it will be down to 25 curies and so on. Other radioactive substances, particularly those synthesised under laboratory conditions, have much shorter half-lives measured in days, minutes, seconds or parts of seconds. The reason for referring to this particular measure is that the rate of decrease in activity is rapid at first and gradually slowing. This seems to me an accurate reflection of the loss of intensity of a feeling: the rate at which the feeling diminishes is initially rapid but gradually slows down to a residual level that can remain for a long time.

5 The six foci for supervision which Hawkins and Shohet describe are:

1 The session content from the client's perspective.
2 Interventions and strategies of the counsellor.
3 Dynamics of client–counsellor interaction.
4 The counsellor's countertransference responses to the client.
5 The parallel process between the counselling and supervising relationships.
6 The supervisor's countertransference responses to the counsellor.

6 I also go on to ask them to consider which feelings on the list they never feel and invite them to reflect on the possibility that this may (and I stress may) indicate feelings that they deny. This offers another, rather crude, way of trying to access shadow material.

5 Confronting the shadow

1 'Road to Damascus experience' refers to the dramatic conversion of St Paul while travelling along the Damascus road (Jerusalem Bible 1968, Acts 9: 1–6). Paul had been a persecutor of the early Christians up to this event and afterwards became one of the key figures in the development of the Christian community.

2 Nondominant hemisphere brain activity is a complex area of which I have a very limited knowledge. However, it seems clear that different human functions operate within the two hemispheres of the brain. The majority of individuals who are normally right-handed have their rational and functional brain activity located primarily in the left hemisphere, with the reverse being the case for most normally organised left-handed people. Bandler and Grinder (1975) propose a correlation between the nondominant hemisphere and the unconscious. While all this is, I believe, scientifically speculative it does provide an intriguingly plausible explanation for the apparent link between creativity and release of unconscious material.

6 Incorporating the shadow

1 Psychic energy is being used here as the psychological equivalent of potential energy in a chemical reaction which is the amount of energy that may, under favourable conditions, be released. I am offering this as a metaphor for the psychic energetic system in which energy is used in a variety of different forms. Energy that is being used to maintain internal defensive systems is not therefore available for interaction with the external world or for other internal processes.

2 Stoltenburg and Delworth (1987) offer a four-level model for the development of a counsellor with corresponding supervisor interventions and behaviours. The 'novice' or first level describes a counsellor who is anxious and uncertain with much of their attention on themselves and their own performance. It is similar to stage two, 'transition to professional training', of Skovolt and Rønnestad (1995). There is a summary of all four stages of Stoltenberg and Delworth's model in Page and Wosket (1994).

3 Self-assessment is often used in a variety of forms in counselling and therapy training. It involves some form of reflective process, assessing oneself against either implicit or explicit criteria, which are often self-defined. The self-assessment is usually subject to consideration from other course members and tutors. It has a significant advantage in therapeutic training over traditional tutor assessments in that the process of formulating the assessment is a useful vehicle for improving the self-reflective capacity in the trainee.

8 The client: mask, person and shadow

1 Endogenous clinical depression has been used as a term to describe a 'major depressive episode' (APA 1994) which has no discernible relationship with any event in the individual's life. This is distinct from reactive depression where the mood of depression is deemed to be a direct consequence of some event in the person's life, most commonly some form of loss.

9 The shadow of the profession

1 I have chosen to use the term 'collective shadow' rather than 'cultural shadow' simply because there is such complexity in defining what constitutes a culture in contemporary society. For instance, the inhabitants of the United Kingdom could be described as a collective as there is a characteristic common to all those people: their geographical location. However, this same geographical area has people living in it from a diverse range of cultures with divisions along national, ethnic, religious, class and many other lines. The notion of collective is less rich in some ways than culture but in this respect it is simpler and less open to ambiguity.

2 Jung refers to the law of enantiodromia (Samuels *et al.* 1986) which I understand as the inevitable movement of everything towards its opposite. This lies at the heart of the notion of shadow: the inevitable creation in our unconscious aspect of the opposites of those characteristics we emphasise in our conscious selves. Enantiodromia predicts that the shadow moving into consciousness is an inevitable psychological process unless blocked by deep-seated and psychologically costly defences.

3 Jonestown massacre: 900 followers of Revd Jim Jones all committed mutual murder or suicide in Jonestown, Guyana, in 1978. Waco siege: a group of

followers of David Koresh died under ambiguous circumstances in Waco, USA, in 1993. The deaths were initially blamed upon the State forces who were surrounding the premises but later appeared more likely to have been self-inflicted.

4 Casement refers in his notes to a previous article published in 1973 that I have not seen. However, my reading of his note is that while he introduced the notion of the 'supervisory viewpoint' in that previous article the term 'internal supervisor' is new to his 1985 book *On Learning from the Patient*.

5 Jung describes the three essential attributes of the mother archetype as 'her cherishing and nourishing goodness, her orgiastic emotionality and her Stygian depths' (1959a: 158). The dark side of nurturing is expressed either through deprivation, withholding that which is needed, or in providing something which is not nutritious but rather is poisonous.

6 The term 'scapegoat' refers to the Hebrew atonement ritual of sacrificing a goat to atone for the sins of the members of the community: a form of ritual cleansing described in the Bible. Similar practices are found in a range of ancient traditions, attesting to the archetypal quality of this sacrificial process. In the Hebrew tradition two goats are sacrificed, one being slaughtered as an offering to Yahweh 'as a sacrifice for sin' (Jerusalem Bible 1968, Lev. 16: 124). The other goat has all the sins of the community spoken over it and it is asked to bear these faults. This goat, the scapegoat, is then taken alive into the desert where it is left as an offering to Azazel, the demon of the desert.

7 It is arguable that the remarkable scenes that followed the death of Diana, Princess of Wales, in 1997 do represent a change in the degree of emotional competence within British society. However, I suspect that the spontaneous expression of grief by many thousands was a response to someone who had become imbued with an archetypal quality (Jobbins 1998). The willingness to show this grief was a secondary response. Emotional competence is demonstrated more in the daily capacity to be with our felt experience than in any emotional outpouring at a momentous event.

8 Personal computers (PCs) are compact computers suitable for the office or home. A CD-Rom is a reading device fitted in computers that uses a compact disc as a source of a computer program and a source of data for that program. A modem is a device that connects a computer via a telephone line or other cable to another computer or a computer network. It may also be used to enable the computer to be used as a fax terminal. The internet is an international computer network and e-mail is electronic mailing (see n. 3, Ch. 3, p. 150). Software is a general term for computer programs and distinguishes these from the hardware: the machines themselves or the electronics contained therein.

Bibliography

Albee, G.W. (1994) 'The fourth revolution', in D. R. Trent and C. Reed (eds) *Promotion of Mental Health Vol 3*, Aldershot: Avebury.

Alexander, J., Kolodziejski, K., Sanville, J. and Shaw, R. (1989) 'On final termination: consultation with a dying therapist', *Clinical Social Work Journal* 17(4): 307–24.

Allen, L. (1990) 'A client's experience of failure', in D. Mearns and W. Dryden (eds) *Experiences of Counselling in Action*, London: Sage.

APA (1994) *Diagnostic Criteria from DSM-IV*, Washington: American Psychiatric Association.

Asper-Bruggisser, K. (1987) 'Shadow aspects of narcissistic disorders and their therapeutic treatment', *Journal of Analytic Psychology* 32: 117–37.

Aveline, M. (1990) 'The training and supervision of individual therapists', in W. Dryden (ed.) *Individual Therapy: A Handbook*, Milton Keynes: Open University Press.

BAC (1997) *Code of Ethics and Practice for Counsellors*, Rugby: British Association for Counselling.

Badaines, A. (1988) 'Psychodrama', in J. Rowan and W. Dryden (eds) *Innovative Therapy in Britain*, Milton Keynes: Open University Press.

Baker, L.C. and Patterson J.E. (1990) 'The first to know: a systematic analysis of confidentiality and the therapist's family', *The American Journal of Family Therapy* 18(3): 295–300.

Bandler, R. and Grinder, J. (1975) *Patterns of the Hypnotic Techniques of Milton H. Erikson, M.D. Volume 1*, Cupertino, CA: Meta.

Barton, A.H. (1969) *Communities in Disaster: A Sociological Analysis of Collective Stress Situations*, London: Ward Lock Educational.

Blocher, D. (1983) 'Towards a cognitive developmental approach to counseling supervision', *The Counseling Psychologist* 11(1): 27–34.

Bly, R. (1988) *A Little Book on the Human Shadow* (edited by William Booth), San Francisco: Harper & Row.

Bollas, C. (1991) *Forces of Destiny: Psychoanalysis and Human Idiom*, London: Free Association Books.

Bollas, C. (1995) *Cracking Up: The Work of Unconscious Experience*, London: Routledge.

Bond, T. (1993) *Standards and Ethics for Counselling in Action*, London: Sage.

Bond, T. (1998) 'Metamorphosis of counselling', in *Counselling and Metamorphosis*, Durham: University of Durham, School of Education.

Bowlby, J. (1988) *A Secure Base*, London: Routledge.

Brandon, D. (1976) *Zen in the Art of Helping*, London: Routledge & Kegan Paul.

Bridges, N.A. and Smith, J.M. (1988) 'The pregnant therapist and the seriously disturbed patient: managing long term psychotherapeutic treatment', *Psychiatry* 51(2): 104–9.

Buber, M. (1970) *I and Thou* (first published 1923), Edinburgh: T and T Clark.

Bugental, J.F.T. (1964) 'The person who is the psychotherapist', *Journal of Counselling Psychology* 28(3): 272–7.

Casement, P. (1985) *On Learning from the Patient*, London: Tavistock.

Castenada, C. (1970) *The Teachings of Don Juan: A Yaqui Way of Knowledge*, Harmondsworth: Penguin.

Clarkson, P. (1989) *Gestalt Counselling in Action*, London: Sage.

Clarkson, P. (1990) 'A multiplicity of psychotherapeutic relationships', *British Journal of Psychotherapy* 7(2): 148–63.

Clothier, C. (1994) *The Allitt Inquiry: An Independent Inquiry Relating to Deaths and Injuries on the Children's Ward at Grantham and Kesteven General Hospital During the Period February to April 1991*, London: HMSO.

Coltart, N. (1993) *How to Survive as a Psychotherapist*, London: Sheldon Press.

Connor, M.P. (1994) *Training the Counsellor*, London: Routledge.

Corey, G. (1995) *Theory and Practice of Group Counseling* (4th edn), California: Brooks/Cole.

Cox, M. (1978) *Structuring the Therapeutic Process: Compromise with Chaos*, Oxford: Pergamon.

Daines, B., Gask, L. and Usherwood, T. (1997) *Medical and Psychiatric Issues for Counsellors*, London: Sage.

Dalley, T. (ed.) (1989) *Art as Therapy: An Introduction to the Use of Art as a Therapeutic Technique*, London: Routledge.

Dass, R. and Gorman, P. (1985) *How Can I Help?*, New York: Alfred A. Knopf.

Douglas, T. (1995) *Scapegoats: Transferring Blame*, London: Routledge.

Dryden, W. (1989) 'The therapeutic alliance as an integrating framework', in W. Dryden *Key Issues for Counselling in Action*, London: Sage.

Dryden, W. (ed.) (1990) *Individual Therapy: A Handbook*, Milton Keynes: Open University Press.

Dryden, W. (1994) 'The Gospel according to St. John', *Self and Society: A Journal of Humanistic Psychology* 22(5): 8–10.

Dryden, W. and Feltham, C. (1992) *Brief Counselling: A Practical Guide for Beginning Practitioners*, Buckingham: Open University Press.

Eckler-Hart, A.H. (1987) 'True and false self in the development of the Psychotherapist', *Psychotherapy* 24(4): 683–92.

Enns, C.Z. (1996) 'Counsellors and the backlash – rape hype and false memory syndrome', *Journal of Counseling and Development* 74(4): 358–67.

Erikson, E. (1977) *Childhood and Society*, St Albans: Paladin.

Fairbairn, W.R.D. (1940) 'Schizoid factors in the personality', in W. R. D. Fairburn (1994) *Psychoanalytic Studies of the Personality*, London: Routledge.

Farber, B.A., (ed.) (1983) *Stress and Burnout in the Human Service Professions*, New York: Pergamon.

Ferrucci, P. (1982) *What We May Be: The Visions and Techniques of Psychosynthesis*, Wellingborough: Turnstone Press.

Fordham, M. (1960) 'Countertransference', in M. Fordham, R. Gordon, J. Hubback and K. Lambert (1974) *Technique in Jungian Analysis* (The Library of Analytical Psychology Volume 2), London: Heinemann.

Fordham, M. (1986) *Jungian Psychotherapy: A Study in Analytical Psychology*, London: Maresfield.

Fossum, M.A. and Mason, M.J. (1986) *Facing Shame: Families in Recovery*, New York: W. W. Norton & Company.

Foulkes, S.H. and Anthony, E.J. (1984) *Group Psychotherapy: The Psychoanalytic Approach*, London: Maresfield.

Frankland, A. (1996) 'Exploring accreditation', in S. Palmer, S. Dainow and P. Milner *Counselling: The BAC Counselling Reader*, London: Sage, in conjunction with The British Association for Counselling.

Freud, S. (1985) 'Totem and taboo', in *The Origins of Religion* (first published 1913), London: Penguin.

Gaultiere, W.J. (1990) 'The Christian psychotherapist as a transitional object to God', *Journal of Psychology and Theology* 18(2): 131–40.

Gerstl, J.E. (1969) 'Counseling and psychotherapy today: role specialisation and diversity', in D. A. Hansen (ed.) *Explorations in Sociology and Counseling*, Boston, MA: Houghton Mifflin.

Gilbert, P., Hughes, W. and Dryden, W. (1989) 'The therapist as a crucial variable in psychotherapy', in W. Dryden and L. Spurling (eds) *On Becoming a Psychotherapist*, London: Routledge.

Goffman, E. (1963) *Stigma: Notes on the Management of Spoiled Identity*, Harmondsworth: Pelican.

Gold, J. and Nemiah, J.(eds) (1993) *Beyond Transference: When the Therapist's Real Life Intrudes*, Washington: American Psychiatric Press

Goldberg, C. (1986) *On Being a Psychotherapist*, New Jersey: Jason Aronson.

Grater, H.A. (1985) 'Stages in psychotherapy supervision: from therapy skills to skilled therapist', *Professional Psychology: Research and Practice*, 16: 605–10.

Graves, R. (1960) *The Greek Myths Volume 1*, London: Penguin.

Gray, A. (1994) *An Introduction to the Therapeutic Frame*, London: Routledge.

Greenson, R.R. (1967) *The Technique and Practice of Psycho-Analysis, Volume 1*, London: The Hogarth Press and Institute of Psycho-Analysis.

Guggenbühl-Craig, A. (1971) *Power in the Helping Professions*, Dallas: Spring.

Guy J.D. (1987) *The Personal Life of the Psychotherapist*, New York: John Wiley & Sons.

Hall, J. (1993) *The Reluctant Adult*, Dorset: Prism Press.

Handy, C.B. (1985) *Understanding Organisations*, Harmondsworth: Penguin.

Hawkins, P. and Shohet, R. (1989) *Supervision in the Helping Professions*, Milton Keynes: Open University Press.

Henry, W. (1966) 'Some observations on the lives of healers', *Human Development* 9: 47–56.

Heppner, P.P. (1989) 'Chance and choices in becoming a therapist', in W. Dryden and L. Spurling (eds) *On Becoming a Psychotherapist*, London: Routledge.

Herbert, F. (1976) *Dune, Dune Messiah, Children of Dune*, London: New English Library.

Heron, J. (1989) *The Facilitators' Handbook*, London: Kogan Page.

Heron, J. (1990) *Helping the Client: A Creative Practical Guide*, London: Sage.

Heron, J. (1992) *Feeling and Personhood: Psychology in Another Key*, London: Sage.

Hess, A.K. (1987) 'Psychotherapy supervision: stages, Buber, and a theory of relationship', *Professional Psychology* 18: 251–9.

Hillman, J. (1979) *Insearch: Psychology and Religion*, Dallas: Spring.

Hillman, J. (1990) *The Essential James Hillman: A Blue Fire*, London: Routledge.

Hillman, J. and Ventura, M. (1992) *We've Had a Hundred Years of Psychotherapy and the World's Getting Worse*, San Francisco: Harper San Francisco/HarperCollins.

Hogan, R.A. (1964) 'Issues and approaches in supervision', *Psychotherapy: Theory, Research and Practice* 1: 139–41.

Holroyd, J.C. and Brodsky, A.M. (1977) 'Psychologists' attitudes and practices regarding erotic and non erotic physical contact with patients', *American Psychologist* 32: 843–9.

Hooper, D. and Dryden, W. (eds) (1991) *Couple Therapy: A Handbook*, Milton Keynes: Open University Press.

Horowitz, M.J. (1989) *Introduction to Psychodynamics: A New Synthesis*, London: Routledge.

Horton, I., Bayne, R. and Bimrose, J. (1995) 'New directions in counselling: a roundtable', *Counselling: the Journal of The British Association for Counselling* 6(1): 34–40.

Irving, J.A. and Williams, D.I. (1996) 'The role of group work in counsellor training', *Counselling: The Journal of the British Association for Counselling* 7(2): 137–9.

Jacobi, J. (1967) *The Way of Individuation*, New York: Meridian.

Jacobs, M. (1986) *The Presenting Past*, Milton Keynes: Open University Press.

Jacobs, M. (1988) *Psychodynamic Counselling in Action*, London: Sage.

Jacobs, M. (1996) 'Forgiveness and revenge', *Self and Society: A Journal of Humanistic Psychology* 24(2):17–19.

Jacoby, M. (1984) *The Analytic Encounter: Transference and Human Relationship*, Toronto: Inner City Books.

Jacoby, M. (1990) *Individuation and Narcissism: The Psychology of Self in Jung and Kohut*, London: Routledge.

Jagim, R.D., Wittman, W.D. and Noll, J.O. (1978) 'Mental health professionals' attitudes towards confidentiality, privilege, and third party disclosure', *Professional Psychology* 9: 458–66.

Jenkins, P. (1997) *Counselling, Psychotherapy and the Law*, London: Sage.

Jerusalem Bible (1968) *The Jerusalem Bible*, London: Darton, Longman and Todd.

Jobbins, B. (1998) 'Diana: a postscript', *Counselling: The Journal of the British Association for Counselling* 9(1): 13–15.

Johns, H. (1997) 'Self-development: lifelong learning?', in I. Horton and V. Varma *The Needs of Counsellors and Psychotherapists*, London: Sage.

Johnson, R.A. (1991) *Owning Your Own Shadow: Understanding the Dark Side of the Psyche*, San Francisco: HarperCollins.

Johnson, R.A. (1993) *The Fisher King and the Handless Maiden*, San Francisco: HarperCollins.

Jung, C.G. (1959a) *The Archetypes and the Collective Unconscious*, Collected Works Volume 9 part I, London: Routledge & Kegan Paul.

Jung, C.G. (1959b) *Aion*, Collected Works Volume 9 part II, London: Routledge & Kegan Paul.

Jung, C.G. (1966) *The Spirit in Man, Art and Literature*, Collected Works Volume 15, London: Routledge & Kegan Paul.

Jung, C.G. (1969) *The Structure and Dynamics of the Psyche*, Collected Works Volume 8 (2nd edn), London: Routledge & Kegan Paul.

Jung, C.G. (1970) *Civilisation in Transition*, Collected Works Volume 10 (2nd edn), London: Routledge & Kegan Paul.

Jung, C.G. (1971) *Psychological Types*, Collected Works Volume 6, London: Routledge & Kegan Paul.

Jung, C.G. (1977) *The Symbolic Life*, Collected Works Volume 18, London: Routledge & Kegan Paul.

Kaplan, A.H., and Rothman, D. (1986) 'The dying psychotherapist', *American Journal of Psychiatry* 143(5): 561–72.

Kempler, B. (1987) 'The shadow side of self disclosure', *Journal of Humanistic Psychology* 27(1): 109–17.

Kopp, S. (1974) *If You Meet the Buddha on the Road, Kill Him!*, London: Sheldon Press.

Kopp, S. (1977) *Back to One: A Practical Guide for Psychotherapists*, Palo Alto, CA: Science and Behavior Books.

Kottler, J.A. (1986) *On Being a Therapist*, Jossey-Bass: San Francisco.

Kübler-Ross, E. (1970) *On Death and Dying*, London: Tavistock.

Laidler, K.J. (1963) *Reaction Kinetics (Vol. 1) Homogeneous Gas Reactions*, Oxford: Pergamon.

Lambers, E. (1993) 'When the counsellor shares the client's problem', in W. Dryden (ed.) *Questions and Answers on Counselling in Action*, London: Sage.

Lane, J. (1991) 'The language of the soul' (first published 1980), in John Button, *The Best of Resurgence*, Bideford: Green Books.

Langs, R. (1982) *Psychotherapy: A Basic Text*, New York: Jason Aronson.

Le Guin, U. (1976) 'The ones who walk away from Omelas', in *The Winds Twelve Quarters*, London: Victor Gollancz.

Le Guin, U. (1993) *A Wizard of Earthsea* (first published 1968), London: Penguin.

Lemma, A. (1996) *Introduction to Psychopathology*, London: Sage.

McConnaughy, E.A. (1987) 'The person of the therapist in psychotherapeutic practice', *Psychotherapy* 24(3): 303–14.

MacDonald, G. (1993) 'Defining the goals and raising the issues in mental health promotion', in D.R. Trent and C. Reed (eds) *Promotion of Mental Health Vol. 2*, Aldershot: Avebury.

McLeod, J. (1990) 'The client's experience of counselling and psychotherapy: a review of the research', in D. Mearns and W. Dryden *Experiences of Counselling in Action*, London: Sage.

Marks, R.W. (1967) *The New Physics and Chemistry Dictionary and Handbook*, London: Bantam.

Marmor, J. (1953) 'The feeling of superiority: an occupational hazard in the practice of psychotherapy', *American Journal of Psychiatry* 110: 370–6.

Mearns, D. and Thorne, B. (1988) *Person-Centred Counselling in Action*, London: Sage.

Miller, A. (1987) *The Drama of Being a Child* (first published 1979), London: Virago.

Miller, G.D. and Baldwin, D.C. (1987) 'Implications of the wounded-healer paradigm for the use of the self in therapy', in M. Baldwin and V. Satir (eds) *The Use of Self in Therapy*, London: Howarth Press.

Norcross, J.C. and Prochaska, J.O. (1986) 'Psychotherapist heal thyself – I. The psychological distress and self-change of psychologists, counselors and laypersons', *Psychotherapy* 23(1): 102–14.

Norcross, J.C. and Grencavage, L.M. (1989) 'Eclecticism and integration in counselling and psychotherapy: major themes and obstacles', *British Journal of Guidance and Counselling*, 17(3): 227–47.

Opler, M.K. (1969) 'Cultural myths and some functions of social psychiatry', in D. Hansen (ed.) *Explorations in Sociology and Counseling*, Boston, MA: Houghton Mifflin.

Page, S. (1992) 'A study of aspects of current counselling practise from an ethical perspective', unpublished M.Ed. dissertation, University College of Ripon and York, St John.

Page, S. and Wosket, V. (1994) *Supervising the Counsellor*, London: Routledge.

Pappas, P.A. (1989) 'Divorce and the psychotherapist', *American Journal of Psychotherapy* 43(4): 506–17.

Pope, G.G. (1990) 'Abuse of psychotherapy: psychotherapist-patient intimacy', *Psychotherapy and Psychosomatics* 53: 191–8.

Pope, K.S. (1996) 'Memory, abuse and science – questioning claims about the false memory syndrome epidemic', *American Psychologist* 51(9): 957–74.

Pope, K.S., Levenson, H. and Schover, L.R. (1979) 'Sexual intimacy in psychology training: results and implications of a national survey', *American Psychologist* 34: 682–9.

Progoff, I. (1975) *At a Journal Workshop*, New York: Dialogue House Library.

Pulver S.E. (1970) 'Narcissism: the term and the concept', *Journal of the American Psychoanalytic Association* 18: 319–41.

Racker, H. (1968) *Transference and Countertransference*, London: Hogarth Press.

Racusin, G.R., Abramowitz, S.I. and Winter, W.D. (1981) 'Becoming a therapist: family dynamics and career choice', *Professional Psychology* 12(2): 271–9.

Raskin, N.J. (1978) 'Becoming – a therapist, a person, a partner, a parent, a . . .', *Psychotherapy: Theory, Research and Practice* 15(4): 362–70.

Ridley, C.R. (1995) *Overcoming Unintentional Racism in Counseling and Therapy*, Thousand Oaks, CA: Sage.

Rogers, C.R. (1951) *Client Centred Therapy*, London: Constable.

Rogers, C.R. (1967) *On Becoming a Person*, London: Constable.

Rosenthall, E.S. (1990) 'The therapist's pregnancy: impact on the treatment process', *Clinical Social Work Journal* 18(3): 213–16.

Rowan, J. (1983) *The Reality Game: A Guide to Humanistic Counselling and Therapy*, London: Routledge & Kegan Paul.

Rowan, J. (1988) *Ordinary Ecstasy: Humanistic Psychology in Action* (2nd edn), London: Routledge.

Rowan, J. (1992) 'John Rowan', in W. Dryden (ed.) *Hard Earned Lessons from Counselling in Action*, London: Sage.

Rowan, J. (1994) 'Do therapists ever cure clients?', *Self and Society: A Journal of Humanistic Psychology* 22(5): 4–5.

Ruddell, P. and Curwen, B. (1997) 'What type of help?', in S. Palmer and G. McMahon (eds) *Client Assessment*, London: Sage.

Russell, J. (1993) *Out of Bounds: Sexual Exploitation in Counselling and Therapy*, London: Sage.

Rutter, P. (1989) *Sex in the Forbidden Zone*, London: Mandala.

Samuels, A. (1985) *Jung and the Post-Jungians*, London: Routledge.

Samuels, A., Shorter, B. and Plaut, F. (1986) *A Critical Dictionary of Jungian Analysis*, London: Routledge.

Schwartz-Salant, N. (1982) *Narcissism and Character Transformation: The Psychology of Narcissistic Character Disorders*, Toronto: Inner City Books.

Sedgwick, D. (1994) *The Wounded Healer*, London: Routledge.

Segal, J. (1993) 'Against self-disclosure', in W. Dryden (ed.) *Questions and Answers on Counselling in Action*, London: Sage.

Shah, I. (1974) *The Way of the Sufi*, Harmondsworth: Penguin.

Shainberg, D. (1983) 'Teaching therapists how to be with their clients', in J. Welwood (ed.) *Awakening the Heart*, Boulder, CO: New Science Library.

Sharaf, M.R. and Levinson, D.J. (1964) 'The quest for omnipotence in professional training', *Psychiatry* 10(3): 135–49.

Shohet, R. (1985) *Dream Sharing*, Wellingborough: Turnstone.

Shohet, R. (1992) 'Robin Shohet', in W. Dryden (ed.) *Hard Earned Lessons from Counselling in Action*, London: Sage.

Shohet, R. (1996) 'Forgiveness: introduction', *Self and Society: A Journal of Humanistic Psychology* 24(2): 3–4.

Shohet, R. (1998) 'Revenge and forgiveness in intimate relationships', presentation at Humberside Association for Counselling 1998 Annual Conference, Humberside, United Kingdom.

Silverstone, L. (1997) *Art Therapy the Person-Centred Way: Art and the Development of the Person* (2nd edn), London: Jessica Kingsley.

Skovolt, T.M. and Rønnestad, M.H. (1995) *The Evolving Professional Self: Stages and Themes in Therapist and Counselor Development*, Chichester: John Wiley & Sons.

Soth, M. (1992) 'The gulf in me . . . just how personal is the political?', *Self and Society: European Journal of Humanistic Psychology* 10(1): 35–7.

Stevens, A. (1990) *Archetype: A Natural History of the Self*, London: Routledge.

Stoltenberg, C.D. and Delworth, U. (1987) *Supervising Counselors and Therapists: A Developmental Approach*, San Francisco: Jossey-Bass.

Storr, A. (1968) *Human Aggression*, London: Penguin.

Storr, A. (1990) *The Art of Psychotherapy* (2nd edn), Oxford: Butterworth-Heinemann.

Strasburger, L.H., Jorgenson, L. and Sutherland, P. (1992) 'The prevention of psychotherapist sexual misconduct: avoiding the slippery slope', *American Journal of Psychotherapy* 46(4): 544–55.

Street, E. (1989) 'Challenging the white knight', in W. Dryden and L. Spurling (eds) *On Becoming a Psychotherapist*, London: Routledge.

Strong, S.R. (1968) 'Counselling: an interpersonal influence process', *Journal of Counselling Psychology* 15(3): 215–24.

Tournier, P. (1963) *The Strong and the Weak*, London: SCM Press.

Trayner, B. and Clarkson, P. (1992) 'What happens if a psychotherapist dies?', *Counselling: The Journal of The British Association for Counselling* 3(1): 23–4.

Treacher, A. and Reimers, S. (1994) *User Friendly Family Therapy*, Oxford: Blackwell.

Trower, P., Casey, A. and Dryden, D. (1988) *Cognitive-Behavioural Counselling in Action*, London: Sage.

Tudor, K. (1996) *Mental Health Promotion: Paradigms and Practice*, London: Routledge.

Ullman, M. and Zimmerman, N. (1987) *Working with Dreams*, Wellingborough: Aquarian Press.

Vigne, J. (1991) 'Guru and psychotherapist: comparisons from the Hindu tradition', *The Journal of Transpersonal Psychology* 23(2): 121–37.

Walfish, S. Polifka, J.A. and Stenmark, D.E. (1985) 'Career satisfaction in clinical psychology: a survey of recent graduates, *Professional Psychology: Research & Practice* 16: 576–80.

Ward, M. (1998) 'Therapy as abuse', *Self and Society: A Journal of Humanistic Psychology*, 26(1): 13–16.

Wasdell, D. (1992) 'In the shadow of accreditation', *Self and Society: European Journal of Humanistic Psychology* 10(1): 3–14.

Weiner, M.F. (1978) *Therapist Disclosure: The Use of Self in Psychotherapy*, London: Butterworths.

Welfel, E.R. and Lipsitz, N.E. (1984) 'The ethical behaviour of professional psychologists: a critical analysis of the research', *The Counselling Psychologist* 12(3): 31–41.

Whitaker, D.S. (1985) *Using Groups to Help People*, London: Routledge & Kegan Paul.

Whitmont, E.C. (1991) *The Symbolic Quest: Basic Concepts of Analytical Psychology*, Princeton, NJ: Princeton University Press.

Whitmore, D. (1991) *Psychosynthesis Counselling in Action*, London: Sage.

Widiger, T.A. and Rorer, L.G. (1984) 'The responsible psychotherapist', *American Psychologist* 39(5): 503–15.

Wilber, K. (1979) *No Boundary: Eastern and Western Approaches to Personal Growth*, Boston, MA: New Science Library.

Wilkins, P. (1997) *Personal and Professional Development for Counsellors*, London: Sage.

Winnicott, D.W. (1965) *The Maturational Processes and the Facilitating Environment*, New York: International Universities Press.

Wosket, V. (1990) 'Counsellor motivation: a neglected factor in helping relationships', unpublished MA dissertation, University of Keele.

Wosket, V. (1999) *The Therapeutic Use of Self: Counselling Practice, Research and Supervision*, London: Routledge.

Author index

Subject index

Page numbers in *italics* refer to figures and tables